Alfred Tylor, Sydney B. J Skertchly

Colouration in Animals and Plants

Alfred Tylor, Sydney B. J Skertchly

Colouration in Animals and Plants

ISBN/EAN: 9783337242961

Printed in Europe, USA, Canada, Australia, Japan

Cover: Foto ©Andreas Hilbeck / pixelio.de

More available books at **www.hansebooks.com**

COLOURATION

IN

ANIMALS AND PLANTS.

BY THE LATE

ALFRED TYLOR, F.G.S.

Edited by

SYDNEY B. J. SKERTCHLY, F.G.S.,

LATE OF H.M. GEOLOGICAL SURVEY.

LONDON:

PRINTED BY ALABASTER, PASSMORE, AND SONS,

FANN STREET, ALDERSGATE STREET, E.C.

1886.

LIST OF WOODCUTS.

DESCRIPTION OF PLATES.

PLATE I. *Kallima Inachus*, the Indian Leaf Butterfly.

   p. 28.   Fig. 1. With wings expanded.

              Fig. 2. Two Butterflies at rest, showing their exact resemblance to dead leaves.

      This insect affords one of the best examples of protective resemblance.

PLATE II. Illustration of mimicry in butterflies.

   p. 30.   Fig. 1. Male of *Papilio merope*.

              Fig. 2. Female of   ditto   mimicking Fig. 3.

              Fig. 3. *Danais niavius.*

      On the African continent both species occur, but in Madagascar *D. niavius* is wanting, and the female *P. merope* is coloured like the male.

PLATE III. Fig. 1. *Gonepteryx Cleopatra.*

   p. 40.   Fig. 2. *Gonepteryx rhamni*, male.

                        Note.—The orange spot in Fig. 2 has spread over the wing in Fig. 1.

              Fig. 3. *Vanessa Antiopa.*

              Fig. 4. *Panopœa hirta.*

              Fig. 5. *Acrea gea.*

      These two last belong to widely different genera, but are admirable examples of mimicry.

PLATE IV. Fig. 1. *Leucophasia Sinapis.*

   p. 42.   Fig. 2.   Ditto,   var. *diniensis.*

              Fig. 3. *Anthocaris cardamines*, male.

              Fig. 4.   Ditto,   female.

              Fig. 5. *Anthocaris belemia.*

PLATE IV.	Fig. 6.	*Anthocaris belia.*	
contd.	Fig. 7.	Ditto,	var. *simplonia.*
	Fig. 8.	*Anthocaris eupheno*, female.	
	Fig. 9.	Ditto,	male.
	Fig. 10.	*Anthocaris euphemoides.*	
	Fig. 11.	*Papilio machaon.*	
	Fig. 12.	*Papilio podalirius.*	
	Fig. 13.	*Pieris napi*, summer form.	
	Fig. 14.	Ditto,	winter form.
	Fig. 15.	Ditto,	var. *bryoniæ* (alpine form).
	Fig. 16.	Ditto,	summer form, underside.
	Fig. 17.	Ditto,	winter form, underside.
	Fig. 18.	Ditto,	var. *bryoniæ*, underside.

Figs. 13-18 illustrate admirably the variations of the yellow and black in the same species.

PLATE V.	Fig. 1.	*Araschnia prorsa*, male.	
p. 44.	Fig. 2.	Ditto,	female.
	Fig. 3.	*Araschnia levana*, female.	
	Fig. 4.	Ditto,	male.
	Fig. 5.	*Paragra ægeria.*	
	Fig. 6.	*Araschnia porima.*	
	Fig. 7.	Ditto,	var. *meione.*
	Fig. 8.	*Grapta interrogationis.*	
	Fig. 9.	Ditto.	
	Fig. 10.	Ditto.	
	Fig. 11.	*Papilio Ajax*, var. *Walshii.*	
	Fig. 12.	Ditto,	var. *telamonides.*
	Fig. 13.	Ditto,	var. *Marcellus.*

Figs. 1-5 are all one species ; *levana* being the winter form, *prorsa* the summer form, and *porima* intermediate. Similiarly 6-7 are the same species, *meione* being the southern form. So with 8-9 and 11-13, which are only seasonal varieties. Here we can actually trace the way in which varieties are formed. *See* Weismann's work, cited in the text.

PLATE VI.	*Syncoryne pulchella*, magnified. After Professor Allman. Gymno-
p. 62.	blastic or Tubularian Hydroids. Ray Soc., 1871, pl. vi., figs. 1
	and 3.
	Fig. 1. A planoblast as seen passively floating in the water after liberation.
	Fig. 2. The entire hydrosoma of syncoryne.
	a. The spadix.
	b. The medusæ or planoblasts in various stages of develop- ment.

PLATE VII.

p. 80.
Fig. 1. *Deilephila galii*, immature.
Fig. 2.   Ditto   brown variety, adult.
Fig. 3. *Deilephila euphorbiæ*.
Fig. 4. *Sphinx ligustri*.
Fig. 5. *Deilephila euphorbiæ*, dorsal view.
Fig. 6. *Orgyia antiqua*.
Fig. 7. *Abraxas grossulariata*.
Fig. 8. *Bombyx neustria*.
Fig. 9. *Callimorpha dominula*.
Fig. 10. *Euchelia jacobææ*.
Fig. 11. *Papilio machaon*.

SPIDERS.

PLATE VIII.
p. 84.
Fig. 1. *Segestria senoculata*, female.
Fig. 2. *Sparassus smaragdulus*, male.
Fig. 3. *Lycosa piscatoria*, female.
Fig. 4. ———— *andrenivora*, male.
Fig. 5. — ———— ———— female.
Fig. 6. ——— *allodroma*, male.
Fig. 7. ———— *agretyca*, male.
Fig. 8. ——— *allodroma*, female.
Fig. 9. Diagram of *Lycosa*, showing form and position of vessels. After Gegenbaur.
Fig. 10. *Lycosa campestris*, female.
Fig. 11. *Thomisus luctuosus*, male.
Fig. 12. *Salticus scenicus*, female.
Fig. 13. *Lycosa rapax*, female.
Fig. 14. ———— *latitans*, female.
Fig. 15. *Theridion pictum*, female.
Fig. 16. *Lycosa picta*, female.
Fig. 17. ———————— male.

All the above are British species, and copied from Blackwell's "Spiders of Great Britain and Ireland." Ray Soc., 1862.

FISHES.

PLATE IX.
p. 88.
Fig. 1. Windermere Char. *Salmo Willughbii*. A species peculiar to our North of England lakes.
Fig. 2. Perch, *Perca fluviatilis*, showing the modified rib-like markings.

SUNBIRDS.

PLATE X.
p. 90.
Fig. 1. *Nectarinea chloropygia*.
Fig. 2. *Nectarinea christinæ*.
These birds illustrate regional colouration well.

LEAVES.

FLOWERS.

COLOURATION IN ANIMALS AND PLANTS.

CHAPTER I.

INTRODUCTION.

BEFORE Darwin published his remarkable and memorable work on the Origin of Species, the decoration of animals and plants was a mystery as much hidden to the majority as the beauty of the rainbow ere Newton analysed the light. That the world teemed with beauty in form and colour was all we knew; and the only guess that could be made as to its uses was the vague and unsatisfactory suggestion that it was appointed for the delight of man.

Why, if such was the case, so many flowers were "born to blush unseen," so many insects hidden in untrodden forests, so many bright-robed creatures buried in the depths of the sea, no man could tell. It seemed but a poor display of creative intelligence to lavish for thousands of years upon heedless savage eyes such glories as are displayed by the forests of Brazil; and the mind recoiled from the suggestion that such could ever have been the prime intention.

But with the dawn of the new scientific faith, light began to shine upon these and kindred questions; nature ceased to appear a mass of useless, unconnected facts, and ornamentation appeared in its true guise as of extreme importance to the beings possessing it. It was the theory of descent with modification that threw this light upon nature.

This theory, reduced to its simplest terms, is that species, past and present, have arisen from the accumulation by inheritance of minute differences of form, structure, colour, or habit, giving to the individual a better chance, in the struggle for existence, of obtaining food or avoiding danger. It is based on a few well-known and universally admitted facts or laws of nature: namely, the law of multiplication in geometrical progression causing the birth of many more individuals than can survive, leading necessarily to the struggle for existence; the law of heredity, in virtue of which the offspring resembles its parents; the law of variation, in virtue of which the offspring has an individual character slightly differing from its parents.

To illustrate these laws roughly we will take the case of a bird, say, the thrush. The female lays on the average five eggs, and if all these are hatched, and the young survive, thrushes would be as seven to two times as numerous in the next year. Let two of these be females, and bring up each five young; in the second year we shall have seventeen thrushes, in the third thirty-seven, in the fourth seventy-seven, and so on. Now common experience tells us not merely that such a vast increase of individuals does not take place, but can never do so, as in a very few years the numbers would be so enormously increased that food would be exhausted.

On the other hand, we know that the numbers of individuals remain practically the same. It follows, then, that of every five eggs four fail to arrive at maturity; and this rigorous destruction of individuals is what is known as the struggle for existence. If, instead of a bird, we took an insect, laying hundreds of eggs, a fish, laying thousands, or a plant, producing still greater quantities of seed, we should find the extermination just as rigorous, and the numbers of individuals destroyed incomparably greater. Darwin has calculated that from a single pair of elephants nearly nineteen millions would be alive in 750 years if each elephant born arrived at maturity, lived a hundred years, and produced six young—and the elephant is the slowest breeder of all animals.

The struggle for existence, then, is a real and potent fact, and it follows that if, from any cause whatever, a being possesses any power or peculiarity that will give it a better chance of survival over its fellows—be that power ever so slight—it will have a very decided advantage.

Now it can be shown that no two individuals are exactly alike, in other words, that variation is constantly taking place, and that no animal or plant preserves its characters unmodified. This we might have expected if we attentively consider how impossible it is for any two individuals to be subjected to exactly the same conditions of life and habit. But for the proofs of variability we have not to rely upon theoretical reasoning. No one can study, even superficially, any class or species without daily experiencing the conviction that no two individuals are alike, and that variation takes place in almost every conceivable direction.

Granted then the existence of the struggle for existence and the variability of individuals, and granting also that if any variation gives its possessor a firmer hold upon life, it follows as a necessity that the most favoured individuals will have the best chance of surviving and leaving descendants, and by the law of heredity, we know these offspring will tend to inherit the characters of their parents. This action is often spoken of as the preservation of favoured races, and as the survival of the fittest.

The gradual accumulation of beneficial characters will give rise in time to new varieties and species; and in this way primarily has arisen the wonderful diversity of life that now exists. Such, in barest outline, is the theory of descent with modification.

Let us now see in what way this theory has been applied to colouration. The colours, or, more strictly, the arrangement of colours, in patterns is of several kinds, viz. :—

1. *General Colouration*, or such as appears to have no very special function as colour. We find this most frequently in the vegetable kingdom, as, for instance, the green hue of leaves, which, though it has a most valuable function chemically has no particular use as colour, so far as we can see.

2. *Distinctive Colouration*, or the arrangement of colours in different patterns or tints corresponding to each species. This is the most usual style of colouring, and the three following kinds are modifications of it. It is this which gives each species its own design, whether in animals or plants.

3. *Protective Resemblance*, or the system of colouring which conceals the animal from its prey, or hides the prey from its foe. Of this class are the green hues of many caterpillars, the brown tints of desert birds, and the more remarkable resemblances of insects to sticks and leaves.

4. *Mimetic Colouration*, or the resemblance of one animal to another. It is always the resemblance of a rare species, which is the favourite food of some creature, to a common species nauseous to the mimicker's foe. Of this character are many butterflies.

C

5. *Warning Colours*, or distinctive markings and tints rendering an animal conspicuous, and, as it were, proclaiming *noli me tangere* to its would-be attackers.

6. *Sexual Colours*, or particular modifications of colour in the two sexes, generally taking the form of brilliancy in the male, as in the peacock and birds of paradise.

Under one or other of these headings most schemes of colouration will be found to arrange themselves.

At the outset, and confining ourselves to the animal kingdom for the present, bearing in mind the fierce intensity of the struggle for life, it would seem that any scheme of colour that would enable its possessor to elude its foes or conceal itself from its prey, would be of vital importance. Hence we might infer that protective colouring would be a very usual phenomenon; and such we find to be the case. In the sea we have innumerable instances of protective colouring. Fishes that lie upon the sandy bottom are sand-coloured, like soles and plaice, in other orders we find the same hues in shrimps and crabs, and a common species on our shores (*Carcinus mænas*) has, just behind the eyes, a little light irregular patch, so like the shell fragments around that when it hides in the sand, with eyes and light spot alone showing, it is impossible to distinguish it.

The land teems with protective colours. The sombre tints of so many insects, birds and animals are cases in point, as are the golden coat of the spider that lurks in the buttercup, and the green mottlings of the underwings of the orange-tip butterfly. Where absolute hiding is impossible, as on the African desert, we find every bird and insect, without exception, assimilating the colour of the sand.

But if protective colour is thus abundant, it is no less true that colour of the most vivid description has arisen for the sole purpose of attracting notice. We observe this in the hues of many butterflies, in the gem-like humming birds, in sun-birds, birds of paradise, peacocks and pheasants. To see the shining metallic blue of a Brazilian Morpho flashing in the sun, as it lazily floats along the forest glades, is to be sure that in such cases the object of the insect is to attract notice.

These brilliant hues, when studied, appear to fall into two classes, having very diverse functions, namely Sexual and Warning Colours.

Protection is ensured in many ways, and among insects one of the commonest has been the acquisition of a nauseous flavour. This is often apparent even to our grosser senses; and the young naturalist who captures his first crimson-and-green Burnet Moth or Scarlet Tiger, becomes at once aware of the existence of a fetid greasy secretion. This the insectivorous birds know so well that not one will ever eat such insects. But unless there were some outward and visible sign of this inward and sickening taste, it would little avail the insect to be first killed and then rejected. Hence these warning colours—they as effectively signal danger as the red and green lamps on our railways.

It may here be remarked that wherever mimickry occurs in insects, the species mimicked is always an uneatable one, and the mimicker a palatable morsel. It is nature's way of writing "poison" on her jam-pots.

The other class of prominent colours—the Sexual—have given rise to two important theories, the one by Darwin, the counter-theory by Wallace.

Darwin's theory of Sexual Selection is briefly this:—He points out in much detail how the male is generally the most powerful, the most aggressive, the most ardent, and therefore the wooer, while the female is, as a rule, gentler, smaller, and is wooed or courted. He brings forward an enormous mass of well-weighed facts to show, for example, how often the males display their plumes and beauties before their loves in the pairing season, and his work is a long exposition of the truth that Tennyson proclaimed when he wrote:—

" In the spring a fuller crimson comes upon the robin's breast,
In the spring the wanton lapwing gets himself another crest,
In the spring a livelier iris changes on the burnished dove,
In the spring the young man's fancy lightly turns to thoughts of love."

That birds are eminently capable of appreciating beauty is certain, and numerous illustrations are familiar to everyone. Suffice it here to notice the pretty Bower Birds of Australia, that adorn their love arbours with bright shells and flowers, and show as unmistakable a delight in them as the connoisseur among his art treasures.

From these and kindred facts Darwin draws the conclusion that the females are most charmed with, and select the most brilliant males, and that by continued selection of this character, the sexual hues have been gradually evolved.

To this theory Wallace takes exception. Admitting, as all must, the fact of sexually distinct ornamentation, he demurs to the conclusion that they have been produced by sexual selection.

In the first place, he insists upon the absence of all proof that the least attractive males fail to obtain partners, without which the theory must fail. Next he tells us that it was the case of the Argus pheasant, so admirably worked out by Darwin, that first shook his faith in sexual selection. Is it possible, he asks, that those exquisite eye-spots, shaded " like balls lying loose within sockets " (objects of which the birds could have had no possible experience) should have been produced . . . " through thousands and tens of thousands of female birds, all preferring those males whose markings varied slightly in this one direction, this uniformity of choice continuing through thousands and tens of thousands of generations " ? *

As an alternative explanation, he would advance no new theory, but simply apply the known laws of evolution. He points out, and dwells upon, the high importance of protection to the female while sitting on the nest. In this way he accounts for the more sombre hues of the female; and finds strong support in the fact that in those birds in which the male undertakes the household duties, he is of a domestic dun colour, and his gad-about-spouse is bedizened like a country-girl at fair time.

With regard to the brilliant hues themselves, he draws attention to the fact that depth and intensity of colour are a sign of vigour and health—that the pairing time is one of intense excitement, and that we should naturally expect to find the brightest hues then displayed. Moreover, he shows—and this is most important to us—that " the most highly-coloured and most richly varied markings occur on those parts which have undergone the greatest modification, or have acquired the most abnormal development." †

It is not our object to discuss these rival views; but they are here laid down in skeleton, that the nature of the problem of the principles of colouration may be easily understood.

Seeing, then, how infinitely varied is colouration, and how potently selection has modified it, the question may be asked, " Is

* Wallace, Tropical Nature, p. 206.   † Op. cit., p. 206.

it possible to find any general system or law which has determined the main plan of decoration, any system which underlies natural selection, and through which it works"? We venture to think there is ; and the object of this work is to develop the laws we have arrived at after several years of study.

CHAPTER II.

INHERITED MEMORY.

MANY of our observations seemed to suggest a quasi-intelligent action on the part of the beings under examination; and we were led, early in the course of our studies, to adopt provisionally the hypothesis that memory was inherited—that the whole was consequently wiser than its parts, the species wiser than the individual, the genus wiser than the species.

One illustration will suffice to show the possibility of memory being inherited. Chickens, as a rule, are hatched with a full knowledge of how to pick up a living, only a few stupid ones having to be taught by the mother the process of pecking. When eggs are hatched artificially, ignorant as well as learned chicks are produced, and the less intelligent, having no hen instructor, would infallibly die in the midst of plenty. But if a tapping noise, like pecking, be made near them, they hesitate awhile, and then take to their food with avidity. Here the tapping noise seems certainly to have awakened the ancestral memory which lay dormant.

It may be said all this is habit. But what is habit? Is it any explanation to say a creature performs a given action by habit? or is it not rather playing with a word which expresses a phenomenon without explaining it? Directly we bring memory into the field we get a real explanation. A habit is acquired by repetition, and could not arise if the preceding experience were forgotten. Life is largely made up of repetition, which involves the formation of habits; and, indeed, everyone's experience (habit again) shows that life only runs smoothly when certain necessary habits have been acquired so perfectly as to be performed without effort. A being at maturity is a great storehouse of acquired habits; and of these many are so perfectly acquired, *i.e.*, have been performed so frequently, that the possessor is quite unconscious of possessing them.

Habit tends to become automatic; indeed, a habit can hardly be said to be formed until it is automatic. But habits are the result of experience and repetition, that is, have arisen in the first instance by some reasoning process; and reasoning implies consciousness. Nevertheless, the action once thought out, or reasoned upon, requires less conscious effort on a second occasion, and still less on a third, and so on, until the mere occurrence of given conditions is sufficient to ensure immediate response without conscious effort, and the action is performed mechanically or automatically: it is now a true habit. Habit, then, commences in consciousness and ends in unconsciousness. To say, therefore, when we see an action performed without conscious thought, that consciousness has never had part in its production, is as illogical as to say that because we read automatically we can never have learned to read.

The thorough appreciation of this principle is absolutely essential to the argument of this work; for to inherited memory we attribute not only the formation of habits and instincts, but also the modification of organs, which leads to the formation of new species. In a word, it is to memory we attribute the possibility of evolution, and by it the struggle for existence is enabled to re-act upon the forms of life, and produce the harmony we see in the organic world.

Our own investigations had led us very far in this direction; but we failed to grasp the entire truth until Mr. S. Butler's remarkable work, "Life and Habit," came to our notice. This valuable contribution to evolution smoothed away the whole of the difficulties we had experienced, and enabled us to propound the views here set forth with greater clearness than had been anticipated.

The great difficulty in Mr. Darwin's works is the fact that he starts with variations ready made, without trying, as a rule, to account for them, and then shows that if these varieties are beneficial the possessor has a better chance in the great struggle for existence, and the accumulation of such variations will give rise to new species. This is what he means by the title of his work, "The Origin of Species by means of Natural Selection or the Preservation of Favoured Races in the Struggle for Life." But this tells us nothing whatever about the origin of species. As Butler puts it, "Suppose that it is an advantage to a horse to have an especially broad and hard hoof: then a horse born with such a hoof will, indeed, probably survive in the struggle for existence; but he was not born with the larger and harder hoof *because of his subsequently surviving.* He survived because he was born fit—not he was born fit because he survived. The variation must arise first and be preserved afterwards."*

Mr. Butler works out with admirable force the arguments, first, that habitual action begets unconsciousness; second, that there is a unity of personality between parent and offspring; third, that there is a memory of the oft-repeated acts of past existences, and, lastly, that there is a latency of that memory until it is re-kindled by the presence of associated ideas.

As to the first point, we need say no more, for daily experience confirms it; but the other points must be dealt with more fully.

Mr. Butler argues for the absolute identity of the parent and off-spring; and, indeed, this is a necessity. Personal identity is a phrase, very convenient, it is true, but still only a provisional mode of naming something we cannot define. In our own bodies we say that our identity remains the same from birth to death, though we know that our bodily particles are ever changing, that our habits, thoughts, aspirations, even our features, change—that we are no more really the same person than the ripple over a pebble in a brook is the same from moment to moment, though its form remains. If our personal identity thus elude our search in active life, it certainly becomes no more tangible if we trace existence back into pre-natal states. We *are*, in one sense, the same individual; but, what is equally important, we *were* part of our mother, as absolutely as her limbs are part of her. There is no break of continuity between offspring and parent—the river of life is a continuous stream. We judge of our own identity by the continuity which we see and appreciate; but that greater continuity reaching backwards beyond the womb to the origin of life itself is no less a fact which should be constantly kept in view. The individual, in reality, never dies; for the lamp of life never goes out.

For a full exposition of this problem, Mr. Butler's "Life and Habit" must be consulted, where the reader will find it treated in a masterly way.

This point was very early appreciated in our work; and in a paper read before the Anthropological Institute† in the year 1879,

---

* Evolution, Old and New, p. 346.

† On a New Method of Expressing the Law of Specific Change. By A. Tylor.

but not published, this continuity was insisted upon by means of diagrams, both of animal and plant life, and its connection with heredity was clearly shown, though its relation to memory was only dimly seen. From this paper the following passage may be quoted : "If, as I believe, the origin of form and decoration is due to a process similar to the visualising of object-thoughts in the human mind, the power of this visualising must commence with the life of the being. It would seem that this power may be best understood by a correct insight into biological development. It has always excited wonder that a child, a separate individual, should inherit and reproduce the characters of its parents, and, indeed, of its ancestors; and the tendency of modern scientific writing is often to make this obscure subject still darker. But if we remember that the great law of all living matter is, that the child is *not* a separate individual, but a part of the living body of the parent, up to a certain date, when it assumes a separate existence, then we can comprehend how living beings inherit ancestral characters, for they are parts of one continuous series in which not a single break has existed or can ever take place. Just as the wave-form over a pebble in a stream remains constant, though the particles of water which compose it are ever changing, so the wave-form of life, which is heredity, remains constant, though the bodies which exhibit it are continually changing. The retrospection of heredity and memory, and the prospection of thought, are well shown in Mrs. Meritt's beautiful diagram."

This passage illustrates how parallel our thoughts were to Mr. Butler's, whose work we did not then know. What we did not see at the time was, that the power of thinking or memory might antedate birth. It is quite impossible adequately to express our sense of admiration of Mr. Butler's work.

Granting then the physical identity of offspring and parent, the doctrine of heredity becomes plain. The child becomes like the parent, because it is placed in almost identical circumstances to those of its parent, and is indeed part of that parent. If memory be possessed by all living matter, and this is what we now believe, we can clearly see how heredity acts. The embryo develops into a man like its parent, because human embryos have gone through this process many times—till they are unconscious of the action, they know how to proceed so thoroughly.

Darwin, after deeply pondering over the phenomena of growth,

D

repair of waste and injury, heredity and kindred matters, advanced what he wisely called a provisional hypothesis—pangenesis.

"I have been led," he remarks, "or, rather, forced, to form a view which to a certain extent, connects these facts by a tangible method. Everyone would wish to explain to himself even in an imperfect manner, how it is possible for a character possessed by some remote ancestor suddenly to reappear in the offspring ; how the effects of increased or decreased use of a limb can be transmitted to the child; how the male sexual element can act, not solely on the ovules, but occasionally on the mother form ; how a hybrid can be produced by the union of the cellular tissue of two plants independently of the organs of generation ; how a limb can be reproduced on the exact line of amputation, with neither too much nor too little added; how the same organism may be produced by such widely different processes as budding and true seminal generation ; and, lastly, how of two allied forms, one passes in the course of its development through the most complex metamorphoses, and the other does not do so, though when mature both are alike in every detail of structure. I am aware that my view is merely a provisional hypothesis or speculation ; but until a better one be advanced, it will serve to bring together a multitude of facts which are at present left disconnected by any efficient cause.*

After showing in detail that the body is made up of an infinite number of units, each of which is a centre of more or less independent action, he proceeds as follows :—

"It is universally admitted that the cells or units of the body increase by self-division or proliferation, retaining the same nature, and that they ultimately become converted into the various tissues of the substances of the body. But besides this means of increase I assume that the units throw off minute granules, which are dispersed throughout the whole system ; that these, when supplied with proper nutriment, multiply by self-division, and are ultimately developed into units like those from which they were originally derived. These granules may be called gemmules. They are collected from all parts of the system to constitute the sexual elements, and their development in the next generations forms a new being; but they are likewise capable of transmission in a dormant state to future generations, and may then be developed. Their development depends on their union with other partially

* Animals and Plants under Domestication, vol. ii., p. 350.

developed or nascent cells, which precede them in the regular course of growth. . . . Gemmules are supposed to be thrown off by every unit; not only during the adult state, but during each stage of development of every organ; but not necessarily during the continued existence of the same unit. Lastly, I assume that the gemmules in their dormant state have a mutual affinity for each other, leading to their aggregation into buds, or into the sexual elements. Hence, it is not the reproductive organs or buds which generate new organisms, but the units of which each individual is composed."*

Now, suppose that instead of these hypothetic gemmules we endow the units with memory in ever so slight a degree, how simple the explanation of all these facts becomes! What an unit has learned to do under given conditions it can do again under like circumstances. Memory *does* pass from one unit to another, or we could not remember anything as men that happened in childhood, for we are not physically composed of the same materials. It is not at all necessary that an unit should remember it remembers any more than we in reading are conscious of the efforts we underwent in learning our letters. Few of us can remember learning to walk, and none of us recollect learning to talk. Yet surely the fact that we do read, and walk, and talk, proves that we have not forgotten how.

Bearing in mind, then, the fundamental laws that the offspring is one in continuity with its parents, and that memory arises chiefly from repetition in a definite order (for we cannot readily reverse the process—we cannot sing the National Anthem backwards), it is easy to see how the oft-performed actions of an individual become its unconscious habits, and these by inheritance become the instincts and unconscious actions of the species. Experience and memory are thus the key-note to the origin of species.

Granting that all living matter possesses memory, we must admit that all actions are at first conscious in a certain degree, and in the "sense of need" we have the great stimulation to action.

In Natural Selection, as expounded by Mr. Darwin, there is no principle by which small variations can be accumulated. Take any form, and let it vary in all directions. We may represent the original form by a spot, and the variations by a ring of dots. Each one of these dots may vary in all directions, and so other rings of

* Animals and Plants under Domestication, vol. ii., p. 370.

dots must be made, and so on, the result not being development along a certain line, but an infinity of interlacing curves. The tree of life is not like this. It branches ever outwards and onwards. The eyes of the Argus pheasant and peacock have been formed by the accumulation, through long generations, of more and more perfect forms; the mechanism of the eye and hand has arisen by the gradual accumulation of more and more perfect forms, and these processes have been continued along definite lines.

If we grant memory we eliminate this hap-hazard natural selection. We see how a being that has once begun to perform a certain action will soon perform it automatically, and when its habits are confirmed its descendants will more readily work in this direction than any other, and so specialisation may arise.

To take the cases of protective resemblance and mimicry. Darwin and Wallace have to start with a form something like the body mimicked, without giving any idea as to how that resemblance could arise. But with this key of memory we can open nature's treasure house much more fully. Look, for instance, at nocturnal insects; and one need not go further than the beetles (*Blatta*) in the kitchen, to see that they have a sense of need, and use it. Suddenly turn up the gas, and see the hurried scamper of the alarmed crowd. They are perfectly aware that danger is at hand. Equally well do they feel that safety lies in concealment; and while all the foraging party on the white floor are scuttling away into dark corners, the fortunate dweller on the hearth stands motionless beneath the shadow of the fire-irons; a picture of keen, intense excitement, with antennæ quivering with alertness. On the clean floor a careless girl has dropped a piece of flat coal, and on it beetles stand rigidly. They are as conscious as we are that the shadow, and the colour of the coal afford concealment, and we cannot doubt that they have become black from their sense of the protection they thus enjoy. They do not say, as Tom, the Water Baby, says, "I must be clean," but they know they must be black, and black they are.

There is, then, clearly an effort to assimilate in hue to their surroundings, and the whole question is comparatively clear.

Mr. Wallace, in commenting upon the butterfly (*Papilio nireus*)—which, at the Cape, in its chrysalis state, copies the bright hues of the vegetation upon which it passes its dormant phase—says that this is a kind of natural colour photography : thus reducing the action to a mere physical one. We might as well say the dun coat

of the sportsman among the brown heather was acquired mechanically. Moreover, Wallace distinctly shows that when the larvæ are
made to pupate on unnatural colours, like sky-blue or vermilion,
the pupæ do not mimic the colour. There is no reason why
"natural photography" should not copy this as well as the greens,
and browns, and yellows. But how easy the explanation becomes
when memory, the sense of need, and Butler's little "dose of
reason," are admitted! For ages the butterfly has been acquainted
with greens, and browns, and yellows, they are every day experiences; but it has no acquaintance with aniline dyes, and therefore
cannot copy them.

The moral of all this is that things become easy by repetition;
that without experience nothing can be done well, and that the
course of development is always in one direction, because the
memory of the road traversed is not forgotten.

CHAPTER III.

INTRODUCTORY SKETCH.

NATURAL science has shown us how the existing colouration of an animal or plant can be laid hold of and modified in almost infinite ways under the influence of natural or artificial evolution.

It shows us, for example, how the early pink leaf-buds have been modified into attractive flowers to ensure fertilisation; and it has tracked this action through many of its details. It has explained the rich hue of the bracts of *Bougainvillea*, in which the flowers themselves are inconspicuous, and the coloured flower-stems in other plants, as efforts to attract notice of the flower-frequenting insects. It has explained how a blaze of colour is attained in some plants, as in roses and lilies by large single flowers; how the same effect is produced by a number of small flowers brought to the same plane by gradually increasing flower-stalks, as in the elderberry, or by still smaller flowers clustered into a head, as in daisies and sun-flowers.

It teaches us again how fruits have become highly coloured to lure fruit-eating birds and mammals, and how many flowers are striped as guides to the honey-bearing nectary.

Entering more into detail, we are enabled to see how the weird walking-stick and leaf-insects have attained their remarkable protective resemblances, and how the East Indian leaf-butterflies are enabled to deceive alike the birds that would fain devour them, and the naturalist who would study them. Even the still more remarkable cases of protective mimicry, in which one animal so closely mimics another as to derive all the benefits that accrue to its protector, are made clear.

All these and many other points have been deeply investigated, and are now the common property of naturalists.

But up to the present no one has attempted systematically to find out the principles or laws which govern the distribution of colouration; laws which underlie natural selection, and by which alone it can work. Natural selection can show, for instance, how the lion has become almost uniform in colour, while the leopard is spotted, and the tiger striped. The lion living on the plains in open country is thus rendered less conspicuous to his prey, the leopard delighting in forest glades is hardly distinguishable among the changing lights and shadows that flicker through the leaves, and the tiger lurking amid the jungle simulates the banded shades of the cane-brake in his striped mantle.

Beyond this, science has not yet gone; and it is our object to carry the study of natural colouration still further: to show that the lion's simple coat, the leopard's spots, and the tiger's stripes, are but modifications of a deeper principle.

Let us, as an easy and familiar example, study carefully the colouration of a common tabby cat. First, we notice, it is darker on the back than beneath, and this is an almost universal law. It would, indeed, be quite universal among mammals but for some curious exceptions among monkeys and a few other creatures of arboreal habits, which delight in hanging from the branches in such a way as to expose their ventral surface to the light. These apparent exceptions thus lead us to the first general law, namely, that colouration is invariably most intense upon that surface upon which the light falls.

As in most cases the back of the animal is the most exposed, that is the seat of intensest colour. But whenever any modification of position exists, as for instance in the side-swimming fishes like the sole, the upper side is dark and the lower light.

The next point to notice in the cat is that from the neck, along the back to the tail, is a dark stripe. This stripe is generally continued, but slighter in character across the top of the skull; but it will be seen clearly that at the neck the pattern changes, and the skull-pattern is quite distinct from that on the body.

From the central, or what we may call the back-bone stripe, bands pass at a strong but varying angle, which we may call rib-stripes.

Now examine the body carefully, and the pattern will be seen to change at the shoulders and thighs, and also at each limb-joint. In fact, if the cat be attentively remarked, it will clearly be seen that the colouration or pattern is *regional*, and dependent upon the structure of the cat.

Now a cat is a vertebrate or backboned animal, possessing four limbs, and if we had to describe its parts roughly, we should specify the head, trunk, limbs and tail. Each of these regions has its own pattern or decoration. The head is marked by a central line, on each side of which are other irregular lines, or more frequently convoluted or twisted spots. The trunk has its central axial backbone stripe and its lateral rib-lines. The tail is ringed; the limbs have each particular stripes and patches. Moreover, the limb-marks are largest at the shoulder and hip-girdles, and decrease downwards, being smallest, or even wanting, on the feet; and the changes take place at the joints.

All this seems to have some general relation to the internal structure of the animal. Such we believe to be the case; and this brings us to the second great law of colouration, namely, that it is dependent upon the anatomy of the animal. We may enunciate these two laws as follows :—

I. THE LAW OF EXPOSURE. Colouration is primarily dependent upon the direct action of light, being always most intense upon that surface upon which the light falls most directly.

II. THE LAW OF STRUCTURE. Colouration, especially where diversified, follows the chief lines of structure, and changes at points, such as the joints, where function changes.

It is the enunciation and illustration of these two laws that form the subject of the present treatise.

In the sequel we shall treat, in more or less detail, of each point as it arises; but in order to render the argument clearer, this chapter is devoted to a general sketch of my views.

Of the first great law but little need be said here, as it is almost self-evident, and has never been disputed. It is true not only of the upper and under-sides of animals, but also of the covered and uncovered parts or organs.

For example, birds possess four kinds of feathers, of which one only, the contour feathers, occur upon the surface and are exposed to the light. It is in these alone that we find the tints and patterns that render birds so strikingly beautiful, the underlying feathers being invariably of a sober grey. Still further, many of the contour feathers overlap, and the parts so overlapped, being removed from the light are grey also, although the exposed part may be resplendent with the most vivid metallic hues. A similar illustration can be found in most butterflies and moths. The upper wing slightly overlaps the lower along the lower margin, and although the entire surface of the upper wing is covered with coloured scales, and the underwing apparently so as well, it will be found that the thin unexposed margin is of an uniform grey, and quite devoid of any pattern.

The law of structure, on the other hand, is an entirely new idea, and demands more detailed explanation. Speaking in the broadest sense, and confining ourselves to the animal kingdom, animals fall naturally into two great sections, or sub-kingdoms, marked by the possession or absence of an internal bony skeleton. Those which possess this structure are known as *Vertebrata*, or backboned animals, because the vertebral-column or backbone is always present. The other section is called the *Invertebrata*, or backboneless animals.

Now, if we take the Vertebrata, we shall find that the system of colouration, however modified, exhibits an unmistakably strong tendency to assume a vertebral or axial character. Common observation confirms this; and the dark stripes down the backs of horses, asses, cattle, goats, etc., are familiar illustrations. The only great exception to this law is in the case of birds, but here, again, the exception is more apparent than real, as will be abundantly shown in the sequel. This axial stripe is seen equally well in fishes and reptiles.

For our present purpose we may again divide the vertebrates into limbed and limbless. Wherever we find limbless animals, such as snakes, the dorsal stripe is prominent, and has a strong tendency to break up into vertebra-like markings. In the limbed animals, on the other hand, we find the limbs strongly marked by pattern, and thus, in the higher forms the system of colouration becomes axial and appendicular.

As a striking test of the universality of this law we may take the cephalopoda, as illustrated in the cuttle-fishes. These creatures are generally considered to stand at the head of the Mollusca, and are placed, in systems of classification, nearest to the Vertebrata;

E

indeed, they have even been considered to be the lowest type of Vertebrates. This is owing to the possession of a hard axial organ, occupying much the position of the backbone, and is the well-known cuttle-bone. Now, these animals are peculiar amongst their class, from possessing, very frequently, an axial stripe. We thus see clearly that the dorsal stripe is directly related to the internal axial skeleton.

Turning now to the invertebrata, we are at once struck with the entire absence of the peculiar vertebrate plan of decoration; and find ourselves face to face with several distinct plans.

From a colouration point of view, we might readily divide the animal kingdom into two classes, marked by the presence or absence of distinct organs. The first of these includes all the animals except the Protozoa—the lowest members of the animal kingdom—which are simply masses of jelly-like protoplasm, without any distinct organs.

Now, on our view, that colouration follows structure, we ought to find an absence of decoration in this structureless group. This is what we actually do find. The lowest Protozoa are entirely without any system of colouring; being merely of uniform tint, generally of brown colour. As if to place this fact beyond doubt, we find in the higher members a tendency to organization in a pulsating vesicle, which constantly retains the same position, and may, hence, be deemed an incipient organ. Now, this vesicle is invariably tinged with a different hue from the rest of the being. We seem, indeed, here to be brought into contact with the first trace of colouration, and we find it to arise with the commencement of organization, and to be actually applied to the incipient organ itself.

Ascending still higher in the scale, we come to distinctly organized animals, known as the *Cœlenterata*; of which familiar examples are found in the jelly-fishes and sea anemones. These animals are characterized by the possession of distinct organs, are transparent, or translucent, and the organs are arranged radially.

No one can have failed to notice on our coasts, as the filmy jelly-fishes float by, that the looped canals of the disc are delicately tinted with violet; and closer examination will show the radiating muscular bands as pellucid white lines; and the sense organs fringing the umbrella are vividly black—the first trace of opaque colouration in the animal kingdom.

These animals were of yore united with the star-fishes and sea-urchins, to form the sub-kingdom Radiata, because of their radiate structure. Now, in all these creatures we find the system of colouration to be radiate also.

Passing to the old sub-kingdom Articulata, which includes the worms, crabs, lobsters, insects, etc., we come to animals whose structure is segmental; that is to say, the body is made up of a number of distinct segments. Among these we find the law holds, rigidly that the colouration is segmental also, as may be beautifully seen in lobsters and caterpillars.

Lastly, we have the Molluscs, which fall for our purpose into two classes, the naked and the shelled. The naked molluscs are often most exquisitely coloured, and the feathery gills that adorn many are suffused with some of the most brilliant colours in nature. The shelled molluscs differ from all other animals, in that the shell is a secretion, almost as distinct from the animals as a house is from its occupant. This shell is built up bit by bit along its margin by means of a peculiar organ known as the mantle—its structure is marginate—its decoration is marginate also.

We have thus rapidly traversed the animal kingdom, and find that in all cases the system of decoration follows the structural peculiarity of the being decorated. Thus in the :—

Structureless protozoa there is no varying colouration.
Radiate animals—the system is radiate.
Segmented „ „ segmental.
Marginate „ „ marginal.
Vertebrate „ „ axial.

We must now expound this great structural law in detail, and we shall find that all the particular ornamentations in their various modifications can be shown to arise from certain principles, namely—

1. The principle of Emphasis,
2. The „ Repetition.

The term *Emphasis* has been selected to express the marking out or distinguishing of important functional or structural regions by ornament, either as form or colour. It is with colour alone that we have to deal.

Architects are familiar with the term emphasis, as applied to the ornamentation of buildings. This ornamentation, they say, should *emphasize*, point out, or make clear to the eye, the use or function of the part emphasized. They recognise the fact that to give sublimity and grace to a building, the ornamentation must be related to the character of the building as a whole, and to its parts in particular.

Thus in a tower whose object or function is to suggest height, the principal lines of decoration must be perpendicular, while in the body of a building such as a church, the chief lines must be horizontal, to express the opposite sentiment. So, too, with individual parts. A banded column, such as we see in Early English Gothic, looks weak and incapable of supporting the superincumbent weight. It suggests the idea that the shaft is bound up to strengthen it. On the other hand, the vertical flutings of a Greek column, at once impress us with their function of bearing vertical pressure and their power to sustain it.

This principle is carried into colour in most of our useful arts. The wheelwright instinctively lines out the rim and spokes and does not cross them, feeling that the effect would be to suggest weakness. Moreover, in all our handicraft work, the points and tips are emphasized with colour.

This principle seems to hold good throughout nature. It is not suggested that the colouration is applied to important parts *in order to* emphasize them, but rather that being important parts, they have become naturally the seats of most vivid colour. How this comes about we cannot here discuss, but shall refer to it further on.

It is owing to this pervading natural principle, that we find the extreme points of quadrupeds so universally decorated. The tips of the nose, ears and tail, and the feet also proclaim the fact, and the decoration of the sense organs, even down to the dark spots around each hair of a cat's feelers, are additional proofs. Look, for instance, at a caterpillar with its breathing holes or spiracles along the sides, and see how these points are selected as the seats of specialized colour, eye-spots and stripes in every variety will be seen, all centred around these important air-holes.

This leads us to our second principle, that of repetition, which simply illustrates the tendency to repeat similar markings in like areas. Thus the spiracular marks are of the same character on each segment.

The principle of repetition, however, goes further than this, and tends to repeat the style of decoration upon allied parts. We see this strongly in many caterpillars in which spiracular markings are continued over the segments which lack spiracles; and it is probably owing to this tendency that the rib-like markings on so many mammals are continued beyond the ribs into the dorsal region.

Upon these two principles the whole of the colouration of nature seems to depend. But the plan is infinitely modified by natural selection, otherwise the result would have been so patent as to need no elucidation.

Natural selection acts by suppressing, or developing, structurally distributed colour. So far as our researches have gone, it seems most probable that the fundamental or primitive colouration is arranged in spots. These spots may expand into regular or irregular patches, or run into stripes, of which many cases will be given in the sequel. Now, natural selection may suppress certain spots, or lines, or expand them into wide, uniform masses, or it may suppress some and repeat others. On these simple principles the whole scheme of natural colouration can be explained; and to do this is the object of the following pages.

Into the origin of the colour sense it is not our province to enlarge; but, it will reasonably be asked, How are these colours of use to the creature decorated? The admiration of colour, the charm of landscape, is the newest of human developments. Are we, then, to attribute to the lower animals a discriminative power greater than most races of men possess, and, if so, on the theory of evolution, how comes it that man lost those very powers his remote ancestors possessed in so great perfection? To these questions we will venture to reply.

Firstly, then, it must be admitted that the higher animals do actually possess this power; and no one will ever doubt it if he watches a common hedge-sparrow hunting for caterpillars. To see this bird carefully seeking the green species in a garden, and deliberately avoiding the multitudes of highly coloured but nauseous larvæ on the currant bushes, arduously examining every leaf and twig for the protected brown and green larvæ which the keen eye of the naturalist detects only by close observation; hardly deigning to look at the speckled beauties that are feeding in decorated safety before his eyes, while his callow brood are clamouring for food—to see this is to be assured for ever that birds can, and do, discriminate colour perfectly. What is true of birds can be shown to be true of other and lower types; and this leads us to a very important conclusion—that colouration has been developed with the evolution of the sense of sight. We can look back in fancy to the far off ages, when no eye gazed upon the world, and we can imagine that then colour in ornamental devices must have been absent, and a dreary monotony of simple hues must have prevailed.

With the evolution of sight it might be of importance that even the sightless animals should be coloured; and in this way we can account for the decoration of coral polyps, and other animals that have no eyes; just as we find no difficulty in understanding the colouration of flowers.

Colour, in fact, so far as external nature is concerned, is all in all to the lower animals. By its means prey is discovered, or foes escaped. But in the case of man quite a different state of things exists. The lower animals can only be modified and adapted to their surroundings by the direct influence of nature. Man, on the other hand, can utilise the forces of nature to his ends. He does not need to steal close to his prey—he possesses missiles. His arm, in reality, is bounded, not by his finger tips, but by the distance to which he can send his bolts. He is not so directly dependent upon nature; and, as his mental powers increase, his dependence lessens, and in this way—the æsthetic principle not yet being awakened—we can understand how his colour sense, for want of practice, decayed, to be reawakened in these our times, with a vividness and power as unequalled as is his mastery over nature—the master of his ancestors.

CHAPTER IV.

COLOUR, ITS NATURE AND RECOGNITION.

THIS chapter will be devoted to a slight sketch of the nature of light and colour, and to proofs that niceties of colour are distinguished by animals.

First, as to the nature of light and colour. Colour is essentially the effect of different kinds of vibrations upon certain nerves. Without such nerves, light can produce no luminous effect whatever; and to a world of blind creatures, there would be neither light nor colour, for as we have said, light and colour are not material things, but are the peculiar results or effects of vibrations of different size and velocity.

These effects are due to the impact of minute undulations or waves, which stream from luminous objects, the chief of which is the sun. These waves are of extreme smallness, the longest being only 226 *ten-millionths* of an inch from crest to crest. The tiny billows roll outwards and onwards from their scource at inconceivable velocities, their mean speed being 185,000 miles in a second. Could we see these light billows themselves and count them as they rolled by, 450 billions (450,000,000,000,000) would pass in a single second, and as the last ranged alongside us, the first would be 185,000 miles away. We are not able, however, to see the waves themselves, for the ocean whose vibrations they are, is composed of matter infinitely more transparent than air, and infinitely less dense. Light, then, be it clearly understood, is not the ethereal billows or waves themselves, but only the effect they produce on falling upon a peculiar kind of matter called the optic nerve. When the same vibrations fall upon a photographic sensitive film, another effect—chemical action—is produced: when they fall upon other matter, heat is the result. Thus heat, light and chemical action are but phases, expressions, effects or results of the different influences of waves upon different kinds of matter. The same waves or billows will affect the eye itself as light, the ordinary nerves as warmth, and the skin as chemical action, in tanning it.

Though we cannot see these waves with the material eye, they are visible indeed to the mental eye; and are as amenable to experimental research as the mightiest waves of the sea. Still, to render this subject clearer, we will use the analogy of sound. A musical note, we all know, is the effect upon our ears of regularly recurring vibrations. A pianoforte wire emits a given note, or in other words, vibrates at a certain and constant rate. These vibrations are taken up by the air, and by it communicated to the ear, and the sensation of sound is produced. Here we see the wire impressing its motion on the air, and the air communicating its motion to the ear; but if another wire similar in all respects is near, it will also be set in motion, and emit its note; and so will any other body that can vibrate in unison. Further, the note of the pianoforte string is not a simple tone, but superposed, as it were, upon the fundamental note, are a series of higher tones, called harmonics, which give richness. Now, a ray of sun-light may be likened to such a note; it consists not of waves all of a certain length or velocity, but of numbers of waves of different lengths and speed. When all these fall upon the eye, the sensation of white light is produced, white light being the compound effect, like the richness of the tone of the wire and its harmonics; or we may look upon it as a luminous chord. When light strikes on any body, part or all is reflected to the eye. If all the waves are thus reflected equally, the result is whiteness. If only a part is reflected, the effect is colour, the tint depending upon the particular waves reflected. If none of the waves are reflected, the result is blackness.

Colour, then, depends upon the nature of the body reflecting light. The exact nature of the action of the body upon the light is not known, but depends most probably upon the molecular condition of the surface. Bodies which allow the light to pass through them, are in like manner coloured according to the waves they allow to pass.

We find in nature, however, a somewhat different class of

colour, namely, the iridescent tints, like mother of pearl or shot silk, which give splendour to such butterflies, as some Morphos and the Purple Emperor. These are called diffraction colours, and are caused by minute lines upon the reflecting surface, or by thin transparent films. These lines or films must be so minute that the tiny light waves are broken up among them, and are hence reflected irregularly to the eye.

Dr. Hagen has divided the colours of insects into two classes, the epidermal and hypodermal. The epidermal colours are produced in the external layer or epidermis which is comparatively dry, and are persistent, and do not alter after death. Of this nature are the metallic tints of blue, green, bronze, gold and silver, and the dead blacks and browns, and some of the reds. The hypodermal colours are formed in the moister cells underlying the epidermis, and on the drying up of the specimen fade, as might be expected. They show through the epidermis, which is more or less transparent. These colours are often brighter and lighter in hue than the epidermal; and such are most of the blues, and greens, and yellow, milk white, orange, and the numerous intermediate shades. These colours are sometimes changeable by voluntary act, and the varying tints of the chameleon and many fishes are of this character.

In this connection, Dr. Hagen remarks, that probably all mimetic colours are hypodermal. The importance of this suggestion will be seen at once, for it necessitates a certain consciousness or knowledge on the part of the mimicker, which we have shown, seems to be an essential factor in the theory of colouration.

This author further says, that "the pattern is not the product of an accidental circumstance, but apparently the product of a certain law, or rather the consequence of certain actions or wants in the interior of the animal and in its development."

This remarkable paper, to which our attention was called after our work was nearly completed, is the only record we have been able to find which recognises a law of colouration.

From what has been said of the nature of light, and the physical origin of colour, we see that to produce any distinct tint such as red, yellow, green, or blue, a definite physical structure must be formed, capable of reflecting certain rays of the same nature and absorbing others. Hence, whenever we see any distinct colour, we may be sure that a very considerable development in a certain

F

direction has taken place. This is a most important conclusion, though not very obvious at first sight. Still, when we bear in mind the numbers of light waves of different lengths, and know that if these are reflected irregularly, we get only mixed tints such as indefinite browns; we can at once see how, in the case of such objects as tree trunks, and, still more, in inanimate things like rocks and soils, these, so-to-say, undifferentiated hues are just what we might expect to prevail, and that when definite colours are produced, it of necessity implies an effort of some sort. Now, if this be true of such tints as red and blue, how much more must it be the case with black and white, in which all the rays are absorbed or all reflected? These imply an even stronger effort, and *a priori* reasoning would suggest that where they occur, they have been developed for important purposes by what may be termed a supreme effort. Consequently, we find them far less common than the others; and it is a most singular fact that in mimetic insects, these are the colours that are most frequently made use of. It would almost seem as if a double struggle had gone on: first, the efforts which resulted in the protective colouring of the mimicked species, and then a more severe, because necessarily more rapid, struggle on the part of the mimicker.

Yet another point in this connection. If this idea be correct, it follows that a uniformly coloured flower or animal must be of extreme rarity, since it necessitates not merely the entire suppression of the tendency to emphasize important regions in colour, but also the adjustment of all the varying parts of the organism to one uniform molecular condition, which enables it to absorb all but a certain closely related series of light waves no matter how varied the functions of the parts. Now, such "self-coloured" species, as florists would call them, are not only rare, but, as all horticulturists know, are extremely difficult to produce. When a pansy grower, for instance, sets to work to produce a self-coloured flower—say a white pansy without a dark eye—his difficulties seem insurmountable. And, in truth, this result has never been quite obtained; for he has to fight against every natural tendency of the plant to mark out its corolla-tube in colour, and when this is overcome, to still restrain it, so as to keep it within those limits which alone allow it to reflect the proper waves of light.

The production of black and white, then, being the acme of colour production, we should expect to find these tints largely used for

KALLIMA INACHUS.

very special purposes. Such is actually the case. The sense organs are frequently picked out with black, as witness the noses of dogs, the tips of their ears, the insertion of their vibrissæ, or whiskers, and so on; and white is the most usual warning or distinctive colour, as we see in the white stripes of the badger and skunk, the white spots of deer, and the white tail of the rabbit.

Colour, then, as expressed in definite tints and patterns, is no accident; for although, as Wallace has well said, "colour is the normal character," yet we think that this colour would, if unrestrained and undirected, be indefinite, and could not produce definite tints, nor the more complicated phenomenon of patterns, in which definite hues are not merely confined to definite tracts, but so frequently contrasted in the most exquisite manner. As we write, the beautiful Red Admiral (*V. atalanta*) is sporting in the garden; and who can view its glossy black velvet coat, barred with vividest crimson, and picked out with purest snow white, and doubt for an instant that its robe is not merely the product of law, but the supreme effort of an important law? Mark the habits of this lovely insect. See how proudly it displays its rich decorations; sitting with expanded wings on the branch of a tree, gently vibrating them as it basks in the bright sunshine; and you know, once and for all, that the object of that colour is display. But softly—we have moved too rudely, and it is alarmed. The wings close, and where is its beauty now? Hidden by the sombre specklings of its under wings. See, it has pitched upon a slender twig, and notice how instinctively (shall we say?) it arranges itself in the line of the branch: if it sat athwart it would be prominent, but as it sits there motionless it is not only almost invisible, *but it knows it;* for you can pick it up in your hands, as we have done scores of times. It is not enough, if we would know nature, to study it in cabinets. There is too much of this dry-bone work in existence. The object of nature is *life;* and only in living beings can we learn how and why they fulfil their ends.

Here, in this common British butterfly, we have the whole problem set before us—vivid colour, the result of intense and long continued effort; grand display, the object of that colour; dusky, indefinite colour, for concealment; and the "instinctive" pose, to make that protective colour profitable. The insect *knows* all this in some way. How it knows we must now endeavour to find out.

In attacking this problem we must ask ourselves, What are the purposes that colouration, and, especially, decoration, can alone subserve? We can only conceive it of use in three ways: first, as protection from its enemies; second, as concealment from its prey; third, as distinctive for its fellows. To the third class may be added a sub-class—attractiveness to the opposite sex.

The first necessity would seem to be distinctness of species; for, unless each species were separately marked, it would be difficult for the sexes to discriminate mates of their own kind, in many instances; and this is, doubtless, the reason why species *are* differently coloured.

But protective resemblance, as in *Kallima*,* the Leaf-butterfly, and mimicry, as in *D. niavius* and *P. merope*,† sometimes so hide the specific characters that this process seems antagonistic to the prime reason for colouration, by rendering species less distinct. Now, doubtless, protective colouring could not have been so wonderfully developed *if the organ of sight were the only means of recognition.* But it is not. Animals possess other organs of recognition, of which, as everyone knows, smell is one of the most potent. A dog may have forgotten a face after years of absence, but, once his cold nose has touched your hand, the pleased whine and tail-wagging of recognition, tells of awakened memories. Even with ourselves, dulled as our senses are, the odour of the first spring violet calls up the past; as words and scenes can never do. What country-bred child forgets the strange smell of the city he first visits? and how vividly the scene is recalled in after years by a repetition of that odour!

But insects, and, it may be, many other creatures, possess sense organs whose nature we know not. The functions of the antennæ and of various organs in the wings, are unknown; and none can explain the charm by which the female Kentish Glory, or Oak Egger moths lure their mates. You may collect assiduously, using every seduction in sugars and lanterns, only to find how rare are these insects; but if fortune grant you a virgin female, and you cage her up, though no eye can pierce her prison walls, and though she be silent as the oracles, she will, in some mysterious way, attract lovers; not singly, but by the dozen; not one now and another in an hour, but in eager flocks. Many butterflies possess peculiar scent-pouches on their wings, and one of these, a *Danais*, is mimicked by several species. It is the possession of these additional powers of recognition that leaves colouration free to run to the

---

* Pl. I., Figs 1-3.   † Pl. II., Figs. 1-3.

extreme of protective vagary, when the species is hard pressed in the struggle for life.

Nevertheless, though animals have other means of recognition, the distinctive markings are, without doubt, the prime means of knowledge. Who, that has seen a peacock spread his glorious plumes like a radiant glory, can doubt its fascination? Who, that has wandered in America, and watched a male humming-bird pirouetting and descending in graceful spirals, its whole body throbbing with ecstasy of love and jealousy, can doubt? Who can even read of the Australian bower-bird, lowliest and first of virtuosi, decorating his love-bower with shells and flowers, and shining stones, running in and out with evident delight, and re-arranging his treasures, as a collector does his gems, and not be certain that here, at least, we have the keenest appreciation, not only of colour, but of beauty—a far higher sense?

It has been said that butterflies must be nearly blind, because they seldom fly directly over a wall, but feel their way up with airy touches. Yet every fact of nature contradicts the supposition. Why have plants their tinted flowers, but to entice the insects there? Why are night-blooming flowers white, or pale yellows and pinks, but to render them conspicuous? Why are so many flowers striped in the direction of the nectary, but to point the painted way to the honey-treasures below? The whole scheme of evolution, the whole of the new revelation of the meanings of nature, becomes a dead letter if insects cannot appreciate the hues of flowers. The bee confines himself as much as possible to one species of flower at a time, and this, too, shows that it must be able to distinguish them with ease. We may, then, take it as proven that the power of discriminating colours is possessed by the lower animals.

CHAPTER V.

THE COLOUR SENSE.

THE previous considerations lead us, naturally, to enquire in what manner the sense of colour is perceived.

In thinking over this obscure subject, the opinion has steadily gathered strength that form and colour are closely allied; for form is essential to pattern; and colour without pattern, that is to say, colour indefinitely marked, or distributed, is hardly decoration at all, in the sense we are using the term. That many animals possess the power of discriminating form is certain. Deformed or monstrous forms are driven from the herds and packs of such social animals as cattle, deer, and hogs, and maimed individuals are destroyed. Similar facts have been noticed in the case of birds. This shows a power of recognising any departure from the standard of form, just as the remorseless destruction of abnormally coloured birds, such as white or piebald rooks and blackbirds, by their fellows, is proof of the recognition and dislike of a departure from normal colouring. Authentic anecdotes of dogs recognising their masters' portraits are on record; and in West Suffolk, of late years, a zinc, homely representation of a cat has been found useful in protecting garden produce from the ravages of birds. In this latter case the birds soon found out the innocent nature of the fraud, for we have noticed, after a fortnight, the amusing sight of sparrows cleaning their beaks on the whilom object of terror. Many fish are deceived with artificial bait, as the pike, with silvered minnows; the salmon, and trout, with artificial flies; the glitter of the spoon-bait is often most attractive; and mackerel take greedily to bits of red flannel. Bees sometimes mistake artificial for real flowers; and both they and butterflies have been known to seek vainly for nourishment from the gaudy painted flowers on cottage wall-papers. Sir John Lubbock has demonstrated the existence of a colour sense in bees, wasps, and ants; and the great fact that flowers are lures for insects proves beyond the power of doubt that these creatures have a very strong faculty for perceiving colour.

The pale yellows and white of night-flowering plants render them conspicuous to the flower-haunting moths; and no one who has ever used an entomologist's lantern, or watched a daddy-long-legs (*Tipula*) dancing madly round a candle, can fail to see that intense excitement is caused by the flame. In the dim shades of night the faint light of the flowers tells the insects of the land of plenty, and the stimulus thus excited is multiplied into a frenzy by the glow of a lamp, which, doubtless, seems to insect eyes the promise of a feast that shall transcend that of ordinary flowers, as a Lord Mayor's feast transcends a homely crust of bread and cheese.

We take it, then, as proven that the colour sense does exist, at least, in all creatures possessing eyes. But there are myriads of animals revelling in bright tints; such as the jelly-fishes and anemones, and even lower organisms, in which eyes are either entirely wanting or are mere eye-specks, as will be explained in the sequel. How these behave with regard to colour is a question that may, with propriety, be asked of science, but to which, at present, we can give no very definite reply. Still, certain modern researches open to us a prospect of being able, eventually, to decide even this obscure problem.

The question, however, is not a simple one, but involves two distinct principles; firstly, as to how colour affects the animal coloured, and, secondly, how it affects other animals. In other words, How does colour affect the sensibility of its possessor? and how does it affect the sense organs of others?

To endeavour to answer the first question we must start with the lowest forms of life, and their receptivity to the action of light; for, as colour is only a differentiation of ordinary so-called white light, we might *a priori* expect that animals would show sensibility to light as distinguished from darkness, before they had the power of discriminating between different kinds of light.

This appears to be the case, for Engelmann has shown[*] that many

---

[*] Pflüger's Archiv. f. d. ges. Phys. Bd. **xxix**, 1882, quoted by Romanes. Mental Evolution, p. 80, 1883. *Op. cit.* p. 80.

of the lowest forms of life, which are almost mere specks of protoplasm, are influenced by light, some seeking and others shunning it.
He found, too, that in the case of *Euglena viridis* it would seek the
light only if it "were allowed to fall upon the anterior part of the
body. Here there is a pigment spot; but careful experiment showed
that this was not the point most sensitive to light, a colourless and
transparent area of protoplasm lying in front of it being found to be
so." Commenting upon this Romanes observes, "it is doubtful
whether this pigment spot is or is not to be regarded as an exceed-
ingly primitive organ of special sense." Hæckel has also made
observations upon those lowest forms of life, which, being simply
protoplasm without the slightest trace of organization, not even
possessing a nucleus, form his division *Protista*, occupying the no-
man's-land between the animal and vegetable kingdoms. He finds
that "already among the microscopic Protista there are some that
love light, and some that love darkness rather than light. Many
seem also to have smell and taste, for they select their food with
great care. . . . Here, also, we are met by the weighty fact that
sense-function is possible without sense organs, without nerves. In
place of these, sensitiveness is resident in that wondrous, structureless, albuminous substance, which, under the name of protoplasm, or
organic formative material, is known as the general and essential
basis of all the phenomena of life."*

Now, whether Romanes be correct in doubting whether the
pigment-spot in Euglena is a sense organ or not, matters little to
our present enquiry, but it certainly does seem that the spot, *with
its accompanying clear space*, looks like such an organ. And when
we are further told that after careful experiment it is found that
Euglena viridis prefers blue to all the colours of the spectrum, the
fundamental fact seems to be established that even as low down as
this the different parts of the spectrum affect differently the body of
creatures very nearly at the bottom of the animal scale. This
implies a certain selection of colour, and, equally, an abstention from
other colours.

It is not part of our scheme, however, to follow out in detail the
development of the organs of special sense, and the reader must be
referred to the various works of Mr. Romanes, who has worked long
and successfully at this and kindred problems. Suffice it to say that
in this and other cases he has been led to adopt the theory of

---

* Quoted by Romanes, *op. cit.* p. 81.

inherited memory, though not, as we believe, in the fulness with which it must ultimately be acquired.

This, however, seems certain, that the development, not only of the sense organs, but of organs in general—that is, the setting aside of certain portions for the performance of special duties, and the modifications of those parts in relation to their special duties, is closely related to the activity of the organism. Thus, we find in those animals, like some of the Cœlenterata, which pass some portion of their existence as free-swimming beings, and the remainder in a stationary or sessile condition, that the former state is the most highly organized. This is shown to a very remarkable degree in the Sea Squirts (Ascidians), a class of animals that are generally grouped with the lower Mollusca, but which Prof. Ray Lankester puts at the base of the Vertebrata.

These animals are either solitary or social, fixed or free; but even when free, have little or no power of locomotion, simply floating in the sea. Their embryos are, however, free-swimming, and some of the most interesting beings in nature. Some are marvellously like young tadpoles, and possess some of the distinctive peculiarities of the Vertebrata. Thus, the body is divided into a head and body, or tail, as in tadpoles. The head contains a large nerve centre, corresponding with the brain, which is produced backwards into a chord, corresponding to the spinal chord. In the head, sense organs are clearly distinguishable; there is a well-marked eye, an equally clear ear, and a less clearly marked olfactory organ. Besides this, the spinal-cord is supported below by a rod-like structure, called the notochord. In the vertebrate embryo this structure always precedes the development of the true vertebral column, and in the lowest forms is persistent through life.

We have thus, in the ascidian larva, a form which, if permanent, would most certainly entitle it to a place in the vertebrate sub-kingdom. It is now an active free-swimming creature, but as maturity approaches it becomes fixed, or floating, and all this pre-figurement of a high destiny is annulled. The tail, with its nervous cord and notochord atrophies, and in the fixed forms, not only do the sense organs pass away, but the entire nervous system is reduced to a single ganglion, and the creature becomes little more than an animated stomach. It is, as Ray Lankester has pointed out, a case of degeneration. In the floating forms, which still possess a

G

certain power of locomotion, this process is not carried to such extremes, and the eye is left.

Now, cases of this kind are important as illustrating the direct connection between an active life and advancement; and they also add indirectly to the view Wallace takes of colouration, namely, that the most brilliant colour is generally applied to the most highly modified parts, and is brightest in the seasons of greatest activity.

But they have a higher meaning also, for they may point us to the prime cause of the divergence of the animal and vegetable kingdoms. In thinking over this matter, one of us ventured to suggest that probably the reason why animals dominate the world, and not plants, is, that plants are, as a rule, stationary, and animals lead an active existence. We can look back to the period prior to the divergence of living protoplasm into the two kingdoms. Two courses only were open to it, either to stay at home, and take what came in its way, or to travel, and seek what was required. The stay-at-homes became plants, and the gad-abouts animals. In a letter it was thus put; "It is a truly strange fact that a free-swimming, sense-organ-bearing animal should degenerate into a fixed feeding and breeding machine. It seems to me that the power of locomotion is a *sine qua non* for active development of type, as it necessarily sharpens the wits by bringing fresh experiences and unlooked-for adventures to the creature. I almost think, and this, I believe may be a great fundamental fact, that the only reason why animals rule the world instead of plants is that plants elected to stay at home, and animals did not. They had equal chances. Both start as active elements; the one camps down, and the other looks about him."

Talking over this question with Mr. Butler, he astonished the writer by quoting from his work, "Alps and Sanctuaries" (p. 196), the following passage :—

"The question of whether it is better to abide quiet, and take advantage of opportunities that come, or to go farther afield in search of them, is one of the oldest which living beings have to deal with. It was on this that the first great schism or heresy arose in what was heretofore the catholic faith of protoplasm. The schism still lasts, and has resulted in two great sects—animals and plants. The opinion that it is better to go in search of prey is formulated in animals; the other—that it is better, on the whole, to stay at home.

and profit by what comes—in plants. Some intermediate forms still record to us the long struggle during which the schism was not yet complete.

"If I may be pardoned for pursuing this digression further, I would say that it is the plants, and not we, who are the heretics. There can be no question about this; we are perfectly justified, therefore, in devouring them. Ours is the original and orthodox belief, for protoplasm is much more animal than vegetable. It is much more true to say that plants have descended from animals than animals from plants. Nevertheless, like many other heretics, plants have thriven very fairly well. There are a great many of them, and, as regards beauty, if not wit—of a limited kind, indeed, but still wit—it is hard to say that the animal kingdom has the advantage. The views of plants are sadly narrow; all dissenters are narrow-minded; but within their own bounds they know the details of their business sufficiently well—as well as though they kept the most nicely-balanced system of accounts to show them their position. They are eaten, it is true; to eat them is our intolerant and bigoted way of trying to convert them: eating is only a violent mode of proselytizing, or converting; and we do convert them—to good animal substance of our own way of thinking. If we have had no trouble we say they have 'agreed' with us; if we have been unable to make them see things from our point of view, we say they 'disagree' with us, and avoid being on more than distant terms with them for the future. If we have helped ourselves to too much, we say we have got more than we can 'manage.' And an animal is no sooner dead than a plant will convert it back again. It is obvious, however, that no schism could have been so long successful without having a good deal to say for itself.

"Neither party has been quite consistent. Whoever is or can be? Every extreme—every opinion carried to its logical end will prove to be an absurdity. Plants throw out roots and boughs and leaves: this is a kind of locomotion; and as Dr. Erasmus Darwin long since pointed out, they do sometimes approach nearly to what is called travelling; a man of consistent character will never look at a bough, a root, or a tendril, without regarding it as a melancholy and unprincipled compromise. On the other hand, many animals are sessile; and some singularly successful genera, as spiders, are in the main liers-in-wait."

This exquisitively written passage the writer was quite unaware of having read, though he possessed and had perused the work quoted, nor can he understand how such an admirable exposition could have escaped notice. Had he read it : had he assimilated it so thoroughly as to be unconscious of its existence ; is this a case of rapid growth of automatism ? He cannot say.

To return to the main point, it would seem that specialization is directly proportionate to activity, and when we compare the infinitely diverse organization of the animal with the comparative simplicity of the vegetable world, this conclusion seems to be inevitable.

CHAPTER VI.

SPOTS AND STRIPES.

BEARING in mind the great tendency to repetition and symmetry of marking we have shown to exist, it becomes an interesting question to work out the origin of the peculiar spots, stripes, loops and patches which are so prevalent in nature. The exquisite eye-spots of the argus pheasant, the peacock, and many butterflies and moths have long excited admiration and scientific curiosity, and have been the subject of investigation by Darwin,[*] the Rev. H. H. Higgins,[†] Weismann,[‡] and others, Darwin having paid especial attention to the subject.

His careful analysis of the ocelli or eye-spots in the Argus pheasant and peacock have led him to conclude that they are peculiar modifications of the bars of colour as shown by his drawings. Our own opinion, founded upon a long series of observations, is that this is not the whole case, but that, in the first place, bars are the result of the coalescence of spots. It is not pretended that a bar of colour is the result of the running together of a series of perfect ocelli like those in the so-called tail of the peacock, but merely that spots of colour are the normal primitive commencement of colouring, and that these spots may be developed on the one hand into ocelli or eye-spots, and on the other into bars or even into great blotches of a uniform tint, covering large surfaces.

Let us first take the cases of abnormal marking as shown in disease. An ordinary rash, as in measles, begins as a set of minute red spots, and the same is the case with small pox, the pustules of which sometimes run together, and becoming confluent form bars,

---

[*] Descent of Man, vol. ii., p. 132.   [†] Quart. Journ. Sci., July 1868, p. 325.
[‡] Studies in the Theory of Descent.

which again enlarging meet and produce a blotch or area abnormally
marked. It was these well-known facts that induced us to re-
examine this question. Colouration and discolouration arise from the
presence or absence of pigment in cells, and thus having, as it were
independent sources, we should expect colour first to appear in spots.
We have already stated, and shall more fully show in the sequel, how
colouration follows structure, and would here merely remark that it
seems as if any peculiarity of structure, or intensified function
modifying structure, has a direct tendency to influence colour. Thus
in the disease known as frontal herpes, as pointed out to us by Mr.
Bland Sutton, of the Middlesex Hospital, the affection is characterized by an eruption on the skin corresponding exactly to the
distribution of the ophthalmic division of the fifth cranial nerve,
mapping out all its little branches, even to the one which goes to the
tip of the nose. Mr. Hutchinson, F.R.S., the President of the
Pathological Society, who first described this disease, has favoured
us with another striking illustration of the regional distribution of
the colour effects of herpes. In this case decolouration has taken
place. The patient was a Hindoo, and upon his brown skin the
pigment has been destroyed in the arm along the course of the
ulnar nerve, with its branches along both sides of one finger and the
half of another. In the leg the sciatic and saphenous nerves are
partly mapped out, giving to the patient the appearance of an
anatomical diagram.[*]

In these cases we have three very important facts determined.
First the broad fact that decolouration and colouration in some cases
certainly follow structure; second, that the effect begins as spots;
thirdly, that the spots eventually coalesce into bands and blotches.

In birds and insects we have the best means of studying these
phenomena, and we will now proceed to illustrate the case more
fully. The facts seem to justify us in considering that starting with
a spot we may obtain, according to the development, either an
ocellus, a stripe or bar, or a blotch, and that between these may have
any number of intermediate varieties.

Among the butterflies we have numerous examples of the development from spots, as illustrated in plates. A good example is
seen in our common English Brimstone (*Gonepteryx rhamni*) Fig. 2,
Plate III. In this insect the male (figured) is of a uniform sulphur

[*] See photographs in Hutchinson's Illustrations of Clinical Surgery.

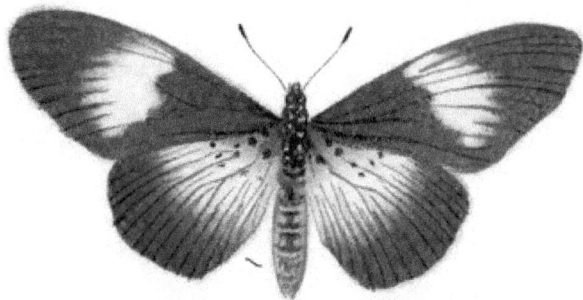

BUTTERFLIES.

yellow, with a rich orange spot in the cell of each wing; the female is much paler in colour, and spotted similarly. In an allied continental species (*G. Cleopatra*) Fig. 1, Plate III., the female is like that of *rhamni* only larger; but the male, instead of having an orange spot in the fore-wing, has nearly the whole of the wing suffused with orange, only the margins, and the lower wings showing the sulphur ground-tint like that of *rhamni*. Intermediate forms between these two species are known. In a case like this we can hardly resist the conclusion that the discoidal spot has spread over the fore-wing and become a blotch, and in some English varieties of *rhamni* we actually find the spot drawn out into a streak.

The family of *Pieridæ*, or whites, again afford us admirable examples of the development of spots. The prevailing colours are white, black and yellow: green *appears* to occur in the Orange-tips (*Anthocaris*), but it is only the optical effect of a mixture of yellow and grey or black scales. The species are very variable, as a rule, and hence of importance to us; and there are many intermediate species on the continent and elsewhere which render the group a most interesting study.

The wood white (*Leucophasia sinapis*) Fig 1, Plate IV., is a pure white species with an almost square dusky tip to the fore-wings of the male. In the female this tip is very indistinct or wanting, Fig. 4, Plate IV. In the variety *Diniensis*, Fig. 2, Plate IV, this square tip appears as a round spot.

The Orange-tips, of which we have only one species in Britain (*Anthocaris cardamines*) belongs to a closely allied genus, as does also the continental genus Zegris. The male Orange-tip (*A. cardamines*) is white with a dark grey or black tip, and a black discoidal spot. A patch of brilliant orange extends from the dark tip to just beyond the discoidal spots. In the female this is wanting, but the dark tip and spot are larger than in the male.

Let us first study the dark tip. In *L. sinapis* we have seen that it extends right to the margin of the wing in the male, but in the female is reduced to a dusky spot away from the margin, In *A. cardamines* the margin is not coloured quite up to the edge, but a row of tiny white spots, like a fringe of seed pearls, occupies the inter-spaces of the veins. On the underside these white spots are prolonged into short bars, see Plate IV. In the continental species *A. belemia* we see the dark tip to be in a very elementary condition, being little more than an irregular band formed of united

spots, there being as much white as black in the tip, Fig. 5, Plate IV.
In *A. belia*, Fig. 6, Plate IV, the black tip is more developed, and in
the variety *simplonia* still more so, Fig. 7, Plate IV. We here see
pretty clearly that this dark tip has been developed by the confluence
of irregular spots.

Turning now to the discoidal spot we shall observe a similar
development. Thus in :—

A. cardamines, male, it is small and perfect.
     Do. female, „ larger „
A. belemia „ large „
A. belia „ large with white centre.
     Do. *v. simplonia* „ small and perfect.
*A. eupheno, female, „ nearly perfect.
     Do. male, „ a band.

We here find two distinct types of variation. In *A. belia* we
have a tendency to form an ocellus, and in *A. eupheno* the spot of
the female is expanded into a band in the male.

The orange flush again offers us a similar case ; and with regard
to this colour we may remark that it seems to be itself a development from the white ground-colour of the family in the direction of
the red end of the spectrum. Thus in the Black-veined white
(*Aporia cratægi*) we have both the upper and under surfaces of the
typical cream-white, for there is no pure white in the family. In the
true whites the under surface of the hind-wings is lemon-yellow, in
the female of *A. eupheno* the ground of the upper surface is faint
lemon-yellow, and in the male this colour is well-developed. The
rich orange, confined to a spot in *G. rhamni* becomes a flush in *G.
Cleopatra*, and a vivid tip in *A. cardamines*. These changes are all
developments from the cream white, and may be imitated accurately
by adding more and more red to the primitive yellow, as the artist
actually did in drawing the plate.

In *A. cardamines* the orange flush has overflowed the discoidal
spot, as it were, in the male, and is absent in the female. But in
A. eupheno we have an intermediate state, for as the figures show, in
the female, Fig. 8, the orange tip only extends half-way to the
discoidal spot, and in the male it reaches it. Moreover it is to be
noticed that the flow of colour, to continue the simile, is unchecked
by the spot in *cardamines*, but where the spot has expanded to a bar in

* See Plate IV.

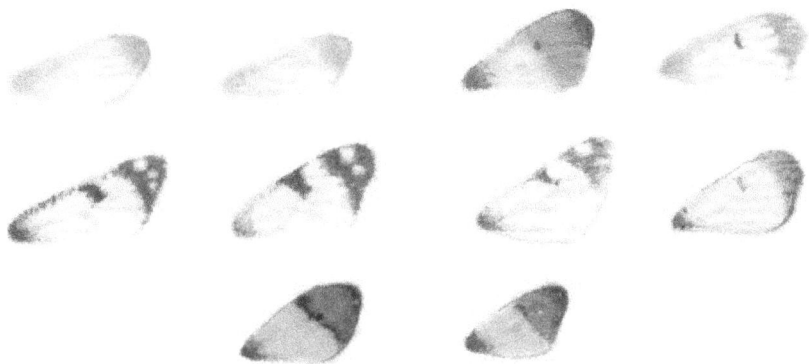

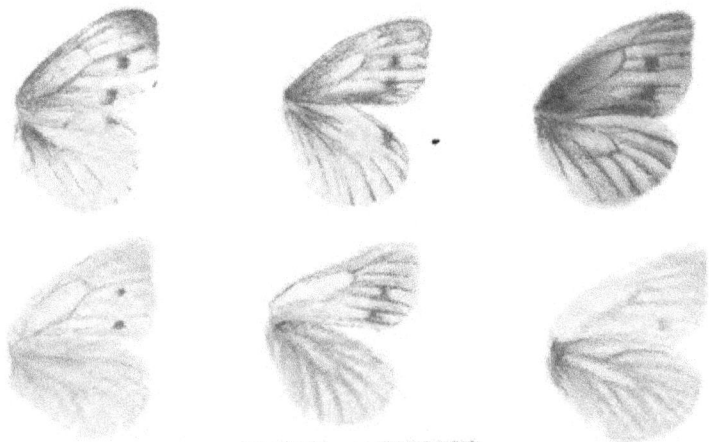

SPOTS AND STRIPES.

eupheno it has dammed the colour up and ponded it between bar and tip. An exactly intermediate case between these two species is seen in *A. euphemoides*, Fig. 10, Plate IV., in which the spot is elongated, and dribbles off into an irregular band, into which the orange has trickled, as water trickles through imperfect fascines. This series of illustrations might be repeated in almost any group of butterflies, but sufficient has been said to show how spots can spread into patches, either by the spreading of one or by the coalescence of several.

We will now take an illustration of the formation of stripes or bars from spots, and in doing so must call attention to the rarity of true stripes in butterflies. By a true stripe I mean one that has even edges, that is, whose sides are uninfluenced by structure. In all our British species such as *P. machaon, M. artemis, M. athalia, V. atalanta, L. sibilla, A. iris,* and some of the Browns, Frittilaries and Hair-streaks, which can alone be said to be striped, the bands are clearly nothing more than spots which have spread up to the costæ, and still retain traces of their origin either in the different hue of the costæ which intersect them, or in curved edges corresponding with the interspaces of the costæ. This in itself is sufficient to indicate their origin. But in many foreign species true bands are found, though they are by no means common. Illustrations are given in Plate IV., of two Swallow-tails, *Papilio machaon*, Fig. 11, and *P. podalirius* Fig 12, in which the development of a stripe can readily be seen.

In *machaon* the dark band inside the marginal semi-lunar spots of the fore-wings retain traces of their spot-origin in the speckled character of the costal interspaces, and in the curved outlines of those parts. In *podalirius* the semi-lunar spots have coalesced into a stripe, only showing its spot-origin in the black markings of the intersecting costæ; and the black band has become a true stripe, with plain edges. Had only such forms as this been preserved, the origin of the spots would have been lost to view.

It may, however, be said, though I think not with justice, that we ought not to take two species, however closely allied, to illustrate such a point. But very good examples can be found in the same species, A common German butterfly, *Araschnia Levana*, has two distinct varieties, *Levana* being the winter, and *prorsa* the summer form; and between these an intermediate form, *porima*, can be bred from the summer form by keeping the pupæ cold. Dr. Weismann, who has largely experimented on this insect, has given accurate illustrations of the varieties. Plate V. is taken from specimens

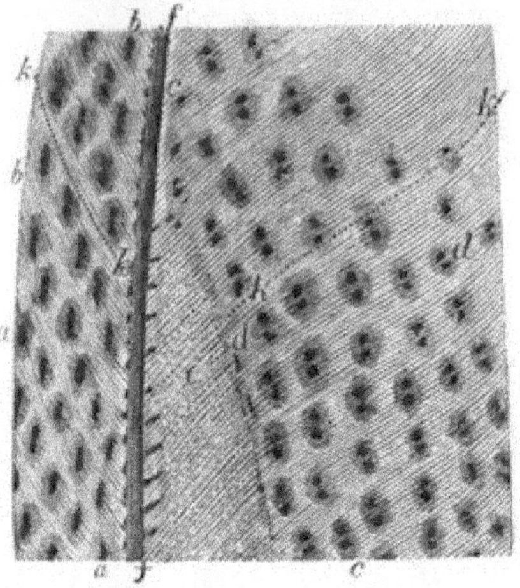

Fig. 1.   Part of secondary feather of Argus Pheasant.

a. a. Elongated spots, incipient   *d. d.* Double spots, incipient ocelli.
     ocelli.   *e.* Minute dottings.
  b. Interspaces.   *f. f.* Shaft.
c. c. Axial line.   *k. k.* Line of feathering.

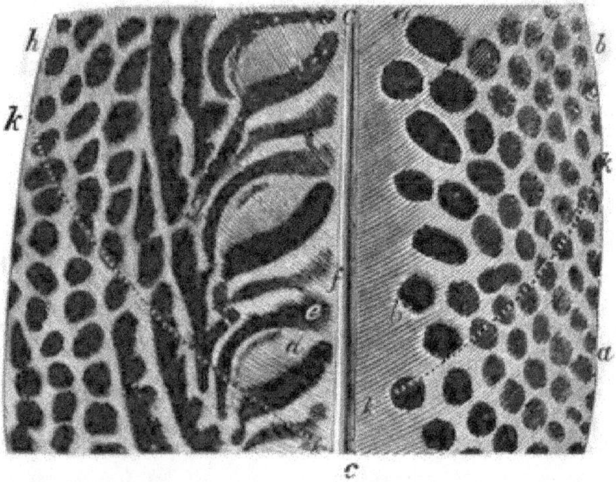

Fig. 2.   Part of secondary wing feather of Argus Pheasant.

a. Oval.   Axis at right angles.   *e.* Expansion of stripe.
b. Round.   *f.* Interspace.
c. c. Shaft.   *g.* Stalk.
d. Imperfect ocellus.   *h.* Edge of feather.
         k. Line of feathering.

SEASONAL VARIETIES.

in our possession. In the males of both *Levana*, Fig. 4, and *prorsa*, Fig. 1, the hind-wing has a distinct row of spots, and a less distinct one inside it, and in the females of both these are represented by dark stripes. In *porima* we get every intermediate form of spots and stripes, both in the male and female, and as these were hatched from the same batch of eggs, or, are brothers and sisters, it is quite impossible to doubt that here, at least, we have an actual proof of the change of spots into stripes.

The change of spots more or less irregular into eye-spots, or ocelli, is equally clear; and Darwin's drawing of the wings of *Cyllo leda** illustrates the point well. "In some specimens," he remarks, "large spaces on the upper surfaces of the wings are coloured black, and include irregular white marks; and from this state a complete gradation can be traced into a tolerably perfect ocellus, *and this results from the contraction of the irregular blotches of colour.* In another series of specimens a gradation can be followed from excessively minute white dots, surrounded by a scarcely visible black line, into perfectly symmetrical and larger ocelli." In the words we have put in italics Darwin seems to admit these ocelli to be formed from blotches; and we think those of the Argus pheasant can be equally shown to arise from spots.

Darwin's beautiful drawings show, almost as well as if made for the purpose, that the bars are developed from spots.† In Fig. 1 is shown part of a secondary wing feather, in which the lines *k. k.* mark the direction of the axis, along which the spots are arranged, perfectly on the right, less so on the left. The lengthening out of the spots towards the shaft is well seen on the right, and the coalescence into lines on the left. In Fig. 2 we have part of another feather from the same bird, showing on the left elongated spots, with a dark shading round them, and on the right double spots, like twin stars, with one atmosphere around them. Increase the elongation of these latter, and you have the former, and both are nascent ocelli. We here, then, have a regular gradation between spots, bands, and ocelli, just as we can see in insects.

In some larvæ, those of the *Sphingidæ* especially, ocelli occur, and these may be actually watched as they grow from dots to perfect eye-spots, with the maturity of the larva.

Even in some mammals the change from spots to stripes can be

* Desc. Man, vol. ii., p. 133, fig. 52.
† Compare his figs. 56 to 58 op. cit.

seen. Thus, the young tiger is **spotted**, and so is the young lion; but, whereas in the former case the **spots** change into the well-known stripes (which are really loops), in the latter they die away. The horse, as Darwin long ago showed, was probably descended from a striped animal, as shown by the bars on a foal's leg. But before this the animal must have been spotted; and the dappled horses are an **example of this**; and, moreover, almost every horse shows a tendency to spottiness, especially on the haunches. In the museum at Leiden a fine series of the Java pig (*Sus vittatus*) is preserved. Very young animals are banded, but have spots over the shoulders and thighs; these run into stripes as the animal grows older; then the stripes expand, and, at last meeting, the mature animal is a uniform dark brown. Enough has now, I trust, been said upon this point to show that from spots have been developed the other markings with which we are familiar in the animal kingdom.

The vegetable kingdom illustrates this fact almost as well. Thus, the beautiful leaves of the Crotons are at first green, with few or no coloured spots; the spots then grow more in number, coalesce, form irregular bands, further develop, and finally cover the whole, or almost the whole, of the leaf with a glow of rich colour. Some of the pretty spring-flowering orchid callitriche have sulphur-yellow petals, with dark rich sepia spots; these often develop to such an extent as to overspread nearly all the original yellow. Many other examples might be given.

Hitherto we have started with a spot, and traced its development. But a spot is itself a developed thing, inasmuch as it is an aggregation of similarly coloured cells. How they come about may, perhaps, be partly seen by the following considerations. Definite colour-pattern has a definite function—that of being seen. We may, therefore, infer that the more definite colour is of newer origin than the less definite. Hence, when we find the two sexes differently coloured, we may generally assume that the more homely tinted form is the more ancient. For example, some butterflies, like the gorgeous Purple Emperor (*Apatura iris*), have very sombre mates; and it seems fair to assume that the emperor's robes have been donned since his consort's dress was originally fashioned.

That the object of brilliant colour is display is shown partly by the fact that in those parts of the wings of butterflies which overlap the brilliant colour is missing, and partly by the generally brighter hues of day-flying butterflies and moths than of the night-flying species. Now, the sombre hues of nocturnal moths are not so much protective (like the sober tints of female butterflies and birds), because night and darkness is their great defender, as the necessary result of the darkness: bright colours are not produced, because they could not be seen and appreciated. In these cases it is very noticeable how frequently the colour is irregularly dotted about—irrorated or peppered over the wings, as it were. This irregular distribution of the pigment cells, if it were quite free from any arrangement, might be looked upon as primitive colouring, undifferentiated either into distinct colour or distinct pattern. If we suppose a few of the pigment cells here and there to become coloured, we should have irregular brilliant dottings, just as we actually see in many butterflies, along the costa. The grouping together of these colour dots would give rise to a spot, from which point all is clear.

That some such grouping or gathering together, allied to segregation, does take place, a study of spots, and especially of eye-spots, renders probable. What the nature of the process is we do not know, nor is it easy to imagine. But let us suppose a surface uniformly tinted brown. Then, if we gather some of the colouring matter into a dark spot we shall naturally leave a lighter area around it, just as we see in all our Browns and Ringlets. In this way we can see how a ring-spot can be formed. To make it a true eye-spot, with a light centre, we must also suppose a pushing away of the colour from that centre. A study of ocelli naturally suggests such a process, which is analogous to the banding of agates, and all concentric nodules. Darwin, struck with this, seems to adopt it as a fact, for he says, " Appearances strongly favour the belief that, on the one hand, a dark spot is often formed by the colouring matter being drawn towards a central point from a surrounding zone, which is thus rendered lighter. And, on the other hand, a white spot is often formed by the colour being driven away from a central point, so that it accumulates in a surrounding darker zone."* The analogy between ocelli and concretions may be a real one. At any rate beautiful ocelli of all sizes can be seen forming in many iron-stained sandstones. The growth of ocelli may thus be a mechanical process adapted by the creature for decorative purposes, but the artistic colouring of many eye-spots implies greater effort.

* Desc. Man, vol. ii., p. 134.

There is, however, one set of colour lines in birds and insects that do not seem to arise from spots in the ordinary way. These are the coloured feather-shafts of birds, and the coloured nerves or veins in a butterfly's wing, In these the colour has a tendency to flow all along the structure in lines.

Conclusion. The results arrived at in this chapter may be thus summarised : —

Spots, ocelli, stripes, loops, and patches may be, and nearly always are, developed from more or less irregular spots.

This is shown both by the study of normal colouring, or by abnormal colouring, or decolouring in disease.

Even the celebrated case of the Argus Pheasant shows that the bands from which the ocelli are developed arose from spots.

CHAPTER VII.

COLOURATION IN THE INVERTEBRATA.

IF the principle of the dependence of colour-pattern upon structure, enunciated in the preceding pages be sound, we ought to find certain great schemes of colouration corresponding to the great structural subdivisions of the animal kingdom. This is just what we do find; and before tracing the details, it will be as well to group the great colour-schemes together, so that a general view of the question can be obtained at a glance.

The animal kingdom falls naturally into two divisions, but the dividing line can be drawn in two ways. If we take the most simple classification, we have :—

1. *Protozoa*, animals with no special organs.
2. *Organozoa*, animals possessing organs.

Practically this classification is not used, but we shall see that from our point of view it is a useful one. In the most general scheme the divisions are :—

1. *Invertebrata*, animals without backbones.
2. *Vertebrata*, animals with backbones.

The invertebrata are divided into sub-kingdoms, of which the protozoa form one. These protozoa possess, as it were, only negative properties. In their simplest form they are mere masses of protoplasm, even lacking an investing membrane or coat, and never, even in the highest forms, possessing distinct organs. It is this simplicity which at once separates them entirely from all other animals.

The other sub-kingdoms are :—

Cœlenterata, of which the jelly-fishes are a type ; animals possessing an alimentary canal, fully communicating with the general cavity of the body, but without distinct circulatory or nervous systems.

Annuloida, of which the star-fishes are a type ; animals having the alimentary canal shut off from the body-cavity, and possessing a nervous system, and in some a true circulatory system.

Annulosa, of which worms, lobsters, and insects are types ; animals composed of definite segments, arranged serially, always possessing true circulatory and nervous systems.

Mollusca, of which oysters and whelks are types ; animals which are soft-bodied, often bearing a shell, always possessing a distinct nervous system and mostly with a distinct heart.

In old systems of classification, the *Cœlenterata* and *Annuloida* were united into one sub-kingdom, the *Radiata,* in consequence of their radiate or star-like structures.

As colouration, according to the views here set forth, depends upon structure, we may classify the Invertebrata thus :—

Protozoa		Structureless.
Cœlenterata ⎱ ... Radiata.		Radiate structure.
Annuloida ⎰		
Annulosa		Segmented „
Mollusca		Marginate „

The mollusca are said to be marginate in structure because, in those possessing shells—the mollusca proper—the shell is formed by successive additions to the margin or edge of the shell, by means of the margin of the mantle, or shell-secreting organ.

Now we shall proceed to show that the schemes of colouration follow out these structure-plans, and thus give additional force to the truth of the classification, as well as showing that, viewed on a broad scale, the present theory is a true one.

We can, in fact, throw the whole scheme into a table, as follows :—

SYSTEMS OF COLOURATION.

	System of Colouring.	Structure.	Sub-kingdoms.
	A. *No Axial Decoration.*	A. *No Axial Structure.*	A. *Invertebrata.*
1.	No definite system.	No definite organs.	Protozoa.
2.	Radiate system.	Radiate structure.	Cœlenterata, Annuloida.
3.	Segmental system.	Segmental structure.	Annulosa.
4.	Marginate system.	Marginate growth.	Mollusca.
	B. *Axial Decoration.*	B. *Axial Structure.*	B. *Vertebrata.*
5.	Axial system.	Axial structure.	Vertebrata.

Protozoa. The protozoa are generally very minute, and always composed of structureless protoplasm. Their peculiarities are rather negative than positive, there being neither body segments, muscular, circulatory, nor nervous systems. Even the denser exterior portion (*ectosarc*) possessed by some of them seems to be rather a temporary coagulation of the protoplasm than a real differentiation of that material.

Here, then, we have to deal with the simplest forms of life, and if colouration depends upon structure, these structureless transparent creatures should lack all colour-pattern, and such is really the case. Possessing no organs, they have no colouration, and are generally either colourless or a faint uniform brown colour, and through their colourless bodies the food particles show, often giving a fictitious appearance of colouring.

To this general statement there is a curious and most telling exception. In a great many protozoa there exists a curious pulsating cell-like body, called the contractile vesicle, which seems to be a rudimentary organ, whose function is unknown. Here, then, if anywhere, traces of colouring should be found, and here it is accordingly found, for, though generally clear and colourless, it sometimes assumes a pale roseate hue. This may be deemed the first attempt at decoration in the animal kingdom, and it is directly applied to the only part which can be said to possess structure. Beautiful examples are plentiful in Leidy's magnificent volume on Freshwater Rhizopods.

Cœlenterata. These animals fall into two groups, the *Hydrozoa*, of which the hydra and jelly-fishes are types, and the *Actinozoa*, of which the sea-anemonies and corals are types. Most of the cœlen-

I

terata are transparent animals, but it is amongst them we first come across opaque colouring.

Of the lowest forms, the hydras, nothing need be said here, as they are so much like the protozoa in their simplicity of structure.

The *Corynida*, familiar to many of our sea-side visitors by their horny brown tubes (*Tubularia*), attached to shells and stones, are next in point of complexity. Within the tube is found a semi-fluid mass of protoplasm, giving rise at the orifice to the polypite, which possesses a double series of tentacles. These important organs are generally of a vivid red colour, thus emphasizing their importance in the strongest manner. Other members of the order are white, with pink stripes.

In the larval stage many of the animals belonging to the above and allied orders, are very like the true jelly-fishes. These free swimming larvæ, or *gonophores*, possess four radiating canals, passing from the digestive sac to the margins of the bell, and these are often the seat of colour. In these creatures, too, we find the earliest trace of sense organs, and consequently, the first highly differentiated organs, and they appear as richly coloured spots on the margins of the bell. The true oceanic Hydrozoa again afford us fine examples of structural colouration. The beautiful translucent blue-purple *Velella*, which is sometimes driven on to our shores, is a case in point; and its delicate structure lines are all emphasized in deeper hues. The true jelly-fishes (*Medusidæ*) with their crystal bells and radiating canals, frequently show brilliant colour, and it is applied to the canals, and also to the rudimentary eye-specks, which are frequently richly tinted, and in all cases strongly marked. In the so-called "hidden-eyed" Medusæ we find the same arrangement of colour, the same emphasized eye-specks, and the reproductive organs generally appear as a vivid coloured cross, showing through the translucent bell.

Turning now to the *Actinozoa*, of which the sea anemonies and corals are types, we are brought first into contact with general decorative, more or less opaque colour, applied to the surface of the animal. In the preceding cases the animals have been almost universally transparent or translucent, and the colouration is often applied to the internal organs, and shows through. In the sea-anemonies we find a nearer approach to opacity, in the dense muscular body, though even this is often translucent, and the tentacles generally so, often looking like clouded chalcedony. The wealth of colour to be found in these animals gives us a very important opportunity of studying decoration, where it first appears in profusion.

One of the first points that strikes even a casual observer is that amongst the sea-anemonies the colouration is extremely variable, even in the same species and in the same locality. This is in strong contrast to what we generally find amongst the higher organisms, such as insects and birds; for though considerable variation is found in them, it does not run riot as in the anemonies. It would almost appear as if the actual colour itself was of minor importance, and only the pattern essential; the precise hue is not fixed, is not important, but the necessity of colour of some sort properly arranged is the object to be attained. Whether this idea has a germ of truth in it or not, it is hard to say, but when we take the fact in connection with its occurrence just where opacity begins, connecting this with the transparency of the lower organisms, and the application of vivid colour to their internal organs, one seems to associate the instability of the anemony's colouring with the transference of colour from the interior to the exterior. Certain it is, that vivid colour never exists in the interior of opaque animals; it is always developed under the influence of light. The white bones, nerves and cartilages, and the uniform red of mammalian muscles, are not cases of true decorative colouring in our sense of the term, for all bodies must have some colour. All bone is practically white, all mammalian muscle red, but for these colours to be truly decorative, it would be necessary for muscles of apparently the same character often to be differently tinted, just as the apparently similar hairs on a mammal, and scales on an insect, are variously painted. This we do not find, for the shaft-bones and plate-bones, and even such odd bones as the hyoid are all one colour; and no one would undertake to tell, by its hue, a piece of striped from a piece of unstriped muscle. Decorative colouring *must* be external in an opaque animal; it *may* be internal in a transparent one.

The connection thus shown between decoration and transparency seems to suggest that hypodermal colour is the original, and epidermal the newer scheme: that the latter was derived from the former. This agrees with Haagen's shrewd hint that all mimetic colour was originally hypodermal. Certain it is that the protective colour that is still under personal control, as in the chameleon, &c., is always hypodermal.

The common crass (*Bunodes crassicornis*) is so extremely variable, that all one can say of it is, that it is coloured red and green. But this colour is distributed in accordance with structure. The base, or crawling surface, not being exposed to the light, is uncoloured. The column, or stem, is irregularly spotted, and striped in accordance with the somewhat undifferentiated character of its tissue, but the important organs, the tentacles, are most definitely ornamented, the colour varying, but the pattern being constant. This pattern is heart-shaped, with the apex towards the point of the tentacle; that is to say, the narrow part of the pattern points to the narrow part of the tentacle.

In the common *Actinea mesembryanthemum*, which is often blood red, the marginal bodies, probably sense-organs, are of the most exquisite turquoise blue colour, and the ruby disc thus beaded is as perfect an example of simple structural decoration as could be desired. A zone of similiar blue runs round the base of the body.

Turning now to the corals, which are simply like colonies of single anemonies with a stony skeleton, we have quite a different arrangement of hues. No sight is more fascinating than that of a living-coral reef, as seen through the clear waters of a lagoon. The tropical gardens ashore cannot excel these sea-gardens in brilliancy or variety of colour. Reds, yellows, purples, browns of every shade, almost bewilder the eye with their profusion; and here again we find structural decoration carried out to perfection. The growing points of white branching corals (*Madrepores*) are frequently tipped with vivid purple, and the tiny polyps themselves are glowing gem-stars. In the white brain-corals, the polyps are vivid red, green, yellow, purple and so on; but in almost every case vividly contrasting with the surrounding parts, the colour changing as the function changes.

The *Alcyonariæ*, which include the sea-fans, sea-pens, and the red coral of commerce, practically bring us to the end of the *Cælenterata*, and afford us fresh proof of the dependence of colour upon structure and function. The well-known organ-pipe coral (*Tubipora musica*) is of a deep crimson colour, and the polyps themselves are of the most vivid emerald green, a contrast that cannot be excelled. Almost equally beautiful is the commercial coral (*Corallium rubrum*) whose vivid red has given a name to a certain tint. In this coral the polyps are of a milk-white colour.

It must be remembered that in these cases the colour seems actually to be intentional, so as to form a real and not merely an accidental contrast between the stony polypidom and the polyp, for the connecting tissue (*cænosarc*) is itself as colourless as it is structureless.

Gathering together the facts detailed in this chapter we find :—

1. That the Protozoa are practically colourless and structureless.
2. That in those species which possess a rudimentary organ (contractile vescicle) a slight decoration is applied to that organ.
3. That in the Cœlenterata the colouration is directly dependent upon the structure.
4. That in transparent animals the colouration is applied directly to the organ whether it be internal as in the canals or ovaries, or external, as in the eye-specks.
5. That in opaque animals, as in the sea-anemonies, the colouring is entirely external.
6. That it is very variable in hue, but not in pattern.
7. That the most highly differentiated parts (tentacles, eye-specks), are the most strongly coloured.
8. That in the corals an emphatic difference occurs between the colour of the polypidom (or " coral ") and the polyp.

CHAPTER VIII.

DETAILS OF PROTOZOA.

THE Protozoa are divided into three orders.

         I.—*Gregarinidæ.*
        II.—*Rhizopoda.*
     III.—*Infusoria.*

I.   The *Gregarinidæ* consist of minute protozoa, parasitic in the interior of insects, &c., and like other internal parasites are colourless, as we should expect.

II.   The *Rhizopoda* may, for our purpose, be divided into the naked forms like *Amœba*, and those which possess a skeleton, such as the Radiolaria, the Foraminifera and the Spongia.

Of these the naked forms are colourless, or uniformly tinted, excepting the flush already described as emphasizing the contractile vesicle.

The *Foraminifera* are the earliest animals that possess a skeleton or shell, and though generally very small, this shell is often complex, and of extreme beauty, though their bodies retain the general simplicity of the protozoa, indeed, they are said to possess no contractile vesicle. Still the complexity of their shells places them on a higher level than the naked rhizopoda.

In these animals we find the first definite colour, not as a pattern, but as simple tinting of the protoplasm. The general hue is yellowish-brown (as in *Amœba*), but deep red is not uncommon. The deepest colour is found in the oldest central chambers, becoming fainter towards the periphery, where it is often almost unrecognisable.*

* Leidy. Rhizopoda of N. America, p. 16.

The *Radiolaria* are minute organisms with still more complex skeletons, and are considered by Haeckel [*] to be more highly organized than the preceding order. They consist of a central portion containing masses of minute cells, and an external portion containing yellow cells. Here we have the first differentiation of parts in the external coating and internal capsule, and side by side with this differentiation we find colour more pronounced, and even taking regional tints in certain forms.

We may notice the following genera as exhibiting fine colour :—

Red. Enceeryphalus, Arachnocorys, Eucrytidium, Dictyoceras
Yellow. Carpocanium, Dictyophimus, Amphilonche.
Purple. Eucrytidium, Acanthostratus.
Blue. Cyrtidosphæra, Cœlodendrum.
Green. Cladococcus, Amphilonche.
Brown. Acanthometra, Amphilonche.

Examples of these may be seen in the plates of Hæckel's fine work, and as an illustration of regional decoration we cite *Acanthostratus purpuraceus*, in which the central capsule is seen to run from red to orange, and the external parts to be colourless, with red markings in looped chains.

Spongocyclia also exhibits this regional distinction of colour very clearly, the central capsule being red and the external portion yellow.

The *Spongida*, or sponges, are, broadly speaking, assemblages or colonies of amœba-like individuals, united into a common society. Individually the component animals are low, very low, in type, but their union into colonies, and the necessity for a uniform or common government has given rise to peculiarities that in a certain sense raise them even above the complex radiolaria. Some, it is true, are naked, and do not possess the skeleton that supports the colony, which skeleton forms what we usually call the sponge; but even amongst these naked sponges the necessity for communal purposes over and above the mere wants of the individual, raises them a step higher in the animal series. A multitude of individuals united by a common membrane, living in the open sea, it must have happened that some in more immediate contact with the food-producing waters, would have thriven at the expense of those in the interior who could only obtain the nutriment that had passed unheeded by the peripheral animals. But just as in higher communities we have an

---

[*] Hæckel. Die Radiolarien, Berlin, 1862.

inflowing system of water and an out-flowing system of effete
sewerage quite uncontrolled, and, alas, generally quite unheeded by
the individuals whose wants are so supplied; so in the sponges we
have a system of inflowing food-bearing water and an out-flowing
sewage, or exhausted-water system. This is brought about by a
peculiar system of cilia-lined cells which, as it were, by their motion
suck the water in, bringing with it the food, and an efferent system
by which the exhausted liquid escapes. These cilia-lined cells are the
first true organs that are to be found in the animal kingdom, and
according to the views we hold, they ought to be emphasized with
colour, even though their internal position renders the colouration
less likely. This we find actually to be the case, and these flagellated cells, as they are called, are often the seat of vividest colour.

The animal matter, or sarcode, or protoplasm of sponges falls
into three layers, just as we find the primitive embryo of the highest
animals; and just as the middle membrane of a mammalian ovum
develops into bone, muscle and nerve, so the middle membrane
(mesosarc) of the sponges develops the hard skeleton, and in this
most important part we find the colour cells prevail. Sollas, one of our
best English authorities upon sponges, writes, " The colours of
sponges, which are very various, are usually due to the presence of
pigment granules, interbedded either in the *endosarc of the flagellated
cells*, or in the mesodermic cells, usually of the skin only, but sometimes of the whole body." *

We can, then, appeal most confidently to the protozoa as illustrating the morphological character of colouration.

* Sollas.   Spongidæ.   Cassell's Nat. Hist. Vol. vi., p. 318.

CHAPTER IX.

Details of Cœlenterata.

I. Hydrozoa.

A. Hydrida.

THE Hydras, as a rule, are not coloured in our sense of the term; that is to say, they are of a general uniform brown colour. But in one species, *H. viridis*, the endoderm contains granules of a green colour, which is said to be identical with the green colouring matter of leaves (*chlorophyll*). This does not occur in all the cells, though it is present in most. The green matter occurs in the form of definite spherical corpuscles, and these colour-cells define the inner layer of the integument (the endoderm), and render it distinct.* That portion of the endoderm which forms the boundary of the body-cavity has fewer green corpuscles, but contains irregular brown granules, thus roughly mapping out a structural region.

We thus see that even in so simple a body as the Hydra the colouring matter is distributed strictly according to morphological tracts.

B. Tubularida. The Tubularian Hydroids are the subject of an exhaustive and admirably illustrated monograph by Prof. J. Allman, from which the following details are culled. These animals are with few exceptions marine, and consist either of a single polypite or of a number connected together by a common flesh, or cœnosarc. Some are quite naked, others have horny tubes, into which, however, the polypites cannot retreat. The polypites consist essentially of a sac surrounded with tentacles; and one of their most striking characters

---

* Allman's Hydroids. Ray. Soc., p. 123.

K

is their mode of reproduction. Little buds (*gonophores*) grow from the cœnosarc, and gradually assume a form exactly like that of a jelly-fish. These drop off, and swim freely about; and are so like jelly-fishes that they have been classed among them as separate organisms.

The Tubulariæ are all transparent; and in them we find structural colouration finely shown, the colour, as is usual in transparent animals, being applied directly to the different organs.

Writing of the colour, Prof. Allman says: "That distinct secretions are found among the Hydroida, and that even special structures are set aside for their elaboration, there cannot now be any doubt.

"One of the most marked of these secretions consists of a coloured granular matter; which is contained at first in the interior of certain spherical cells, and may afterwards become discharged into the somatic fluid. These cells, as already mentioned, are developed in the endoderm;[*] in which they are frequently so abundant as to form a continuous layer upon the free surface of this membrane. It is in the proper gastric cavity of the hydranth and medusa, in the spadix of the sporosac, and in the bulbous dilatations which generally occur at the bases of the marginal tentacles of the medusæ, that they are developed in greatest abundance and perfection; but they are also found, more or less abundantly, in the walls of probably the whole somatic cavity, if we except that portion of the gastrovascular canals of the medusa which is not included within the bulbous dilatations.

"In the parts just mentioned as affording the most abundant supply of these cells, they are chiefly borne on the prominent ridges into which the endoderm is thrown in these situations; when they occur in the intervals between the ridges they are smaller, and less numerous.

"The granular matter contained in the interior of these cells varies in its colour in different hydroids. In many it presents various shades of brown; in others it is a reddish-brown, or light pink, or deeper carmine, or vermilion, or orange, or, occasionally, a fine lemon-yellow, as in the hydranth of *Coppinia arcta*, or even a bright emerald green, as in the bulbous bases of the marginal tentacles of certain medusæ. No definite structure can be detected in it; it is entirely composed of irregular granules, irregular in form,

[*] Compare with Hydra above.

and usually aggregated into irregularly shaped masses in the interior of the cells. It is to this matter that the colours of the *Hydroida*, varying, as they do, in different species, are almost entirely due.

" The coloured granular matter is undoubtedly a product of true secretion; and the cells in which it is found must be regarded as true secreting cells. These cells are themselves frequently to be seen as secondary cells in the interior of parent cells, from which they escape by rupture, and then, falling into the somatic fluid, are carried along by its currents, until, ultimately, by their own rupture, they discharge into it their contents.

" We have no facts which enable us to form a decided opinion as to the purpose served by this secretion. Its being always more or less deeply coloured, and the fact of its being abundantly produced in the digestive cavity, might suggest that it represented the biliary secretion of higher animals. This may be its true nature, but as yet we can assert nothing approaching to certainty on the subject; indeed, considering how widely the cells destined for the secretion of coloured granules are distributed over the walls of the somatic cavity, it would seem not improbable that the import of the coloured matter may be different in different situations; that while some of it may be a product destined for some further use in the hydroid, more of it may be simply excretive, taking no further part in the vital phenomena, and intended solely for elimination from the system."[*]

Here we have very definite statements by a highly trained observer of the distribution of colour in the whole of these animals, and of the conclusions he draws from them.

Firstly as to the colour itself. We find it true colour—brown, pink, carmine, vermilion, orange, lemon-yellow, and even emerald green; a set of hues as vivid as any to be found in the animal kingdom. It is difficult to conceive these granules to be merely excrementitious matter; for in such simple creatures, feeding upon such similar bodies, one would hardly expect the excretive matter to be so diversified in tint. Moreover, excrementitious matter is not, as a rule, highly coloured, but brown. Thus, we see in the Rhizopods the green vegetable matter which has been taken in as food becomes brown as the process of assimilation goes on; and, indeed, colour seems almost always to be destroyed by the act of digestion.

Still, it by no means follows that this colour, even if it is

[*] Allman. Monograph of Tubularian Hydroida. Ray. Soc., p. 135.

produced for the sake of decoration, as we suggest, may not owe its direct origin to the process of digestion. The digestive apparatus is the earliest developed in the animal kingdom, and in these creatures is by far the most important; the cœlenterata being, in fact, little more than living stomachs. If, then, colouration be structural, what is more likely than that the digestive organs should be the seat of decoration in such transparent creatures?

Secondly, as to the distribution of the colour. We find it " frequently forming a continuous layer upon the free surface of " the endoderm, in the " spadix of the sporosac," and in the " bulbous terminations " of the canals, that colour is best developed. In other words, the colour is distributed structurally, and is most strongly marked where the function is most important.

Prof. Allman gives no hint that the colour may be purely decorative, and is naturally perplexed at the display of hues in such vigour; but if this be one of the results of the differentiation of parts, of the specialization of function, then we can, at least, understand why we find such brilliant colour in these creatures, and why it is so distributed.

As an illustration of the *Tubularia* we have selected *Syncoryne pulchella*, Fig. 2, Pl. VI., and its medusa, Fig. 1. The endoderm of the spadix of the hydranths is of a rich orange colour, which becomes paler as it descends towards the less highly organized stem. Medusæ are seen in various stages of development, and one, mature and free, is shown. In these the manubrium, and the bulbous terminations of the canals are also seen to be coloured orange.

In these medusæ we find the first appearance of sensory organs. They consist of pigment-cells enclosed in the ectoderm, or outside covering; and are singular as presenting the first true examples of opaque colouring in the animal kingdom. They are associated with nerve cells attached to a ring of filamentous nerve matter, surrounding the base of the bell. In some important respects the pigment differs from that in other parts of the animal. It is more definite in structure; and the whole ocellus is " aggregation of very minute cells, each filled with a homogeneous coloured matter."* These ocelli, and similar sense organs, called *lithocysts*, are always situated over the bulbous termination of the canals. The pigment is black (as in this case), vermilion, or deep carmine.

* Allman, *op. cit.,* p. 139.

1   2

SYNCORYNE PULCHELLA.

The dependence of colour upon structure is thus shown to hold good throughout these animals in a most remarkable manner, and the acceptance of the views here set forth gives us an insight into the reasons for this colouration which, as we have seen, did not arise from the study of the question from the ordinary point of view.

C. Sertularida. These animals are very similar to the last, but they are all compound, and the polypites can be entirely withdrawn within the leathery investment or polypary. Their mode of reproduction is also similar, and their colouration follows the same general plan. Being so like the preceding order, it is unnecessary to describe them.

B. Siphonophora.

The Siphonophora are all free-swimming, and are frequently called Oceanic Hydrozoa. They are divided into three orders, viz :—

a. *Calycophoridæ.*
b. *Physophoridæ.*
c. *Medusidæ.*

a. *Calycophoridæ.* These animals have a thread-like cœnosarc, or common protoplasm, which is unbranched, cylindrical, and contractile. They are mostly quite transparent, but where colour exists it is always placed structurally. Thus, in *Diphyes* the sacculi of the tentacles are reddish, in *Sphæronectes* they are deep red, and in *Abyla* the edges of the larger specimens are deep blue."[*]

b. *Physophoridæ.* These creatures are distinguished by the presence of a peculiar organ, the float, or *pneumatophore*, which is a sac enclosing a smaller sac. The float is formed by a reflexion of both the ectoderm and endoderm, and serves to buoy up the animal at the surface of the sea. The best known species is the Physalia, or Portuguese Man-o'-War.

Prof. Huxley, in his monograph on the Oceanic Hydrozoa, gives many details of the colouration; and, not having had much opportunity of studying them, the following observations are taken from his work. It will be seen that the Physophoridæ illustrate the structural distribution of colour in a remarkable manner.

Stephanomia amphitridis, the hydrophyllia, colourless, and so

[*] Huxley. Oceanic Hydrozoa, pp. 32, 46, 50.

transparent as to be almost imperceptible in water, cœnosarc whitish, enlarged portions of polypites, pink or scarlet, sacs of tentacles scarlet.

The enlarged portion of the polypites is marked with red striæ, " which are simply elevations of the endoderm, containing thread-cells and coloured granules." The small polypites do not possess these elevations, and are colourless.

Agalma breve, like a prismatic mass of crystal, with pink float and polypites.

Athorybia rosacea, float pink, with radiating dark-brown striæ, made up of dots; polypites lightish red, shading to pink at their apices; tentacles yellowish or colourless, with dark-brown sacculi; thread-cells dark brown.

Rhizophysa filiformis, pink, with deep red patch surrounding the aperture of the pneumatocyst.

Physalia caravilla, bright purplish-red, with dark extremities, and blue lines in the folds of the crest; polypites violet, with whitish points, larger tentacles red, with dark purple acetabula, smaller tentacles blue, bundles of buds reddish.

P. pelagica, in young individuals pale blue, in adult both ends green, with highest part of crest purple, tentacles blue, with dark acetabula; polypites dark blue, with yellow points.

P. utriculus. Prof. Huxley describes a specimen doubtfully referred to this species very fully, as follows :—

" The general colour of the hydrosoma is a pale, delicate green, passing gradually into a dark, indigo blue, on the under surface.

" The ridge of the crest is tipped with lake, and the pointed end is stained deep bluish-green about the aperture of the pneumato-cyst.

" The bases of the tentacles are deep blue; the polypites deep blue at their bases, and frequently bright yellow at their apices; the velvetty masses of reproductive organs and buds on the under surface are light green."

He further remarks that the tentacles have reniform thickenings at regular intervals, and " the substance of each thickening has a dark blue colour, and imbedded within it are myriads of close-set, colourless, spherical thread-cells."

It would not be possible to find a more perfect example of regional colouration. Not only is each organ differently coloured, but the important parts of each organ, like the ridge of the crest, the bases of the tentacles, and the thread-cell bearing ridges of the tentacles, are also emphasized with deep colour.

Velella. This beautiful creature, which sometimes finds its way to our shores, is like a crystal raft fringed with tentacles, and having an upright oblique crest, or sail. The margins of the disk and crest are often of a beautiful blue colour, and the canals of the disk become deep blue as they approach the crest. The polypites may be blue, purple, green, or brown.

C. Medusidæ. The structure and colouration of the true Medusæ are so like that of the medusiform larvæ of the other Hydrozoa, that they need not be particularly described.

D. Lucernarida. Of this sub-class we need only cite the *Lucernaria* themselves; which are pretty bell-shaped animals, having the power of attaching themselves to seaweeds, etc., and also of swimming freely about. Round the margin are eight tufts of tentacles, opposite eight lobes, the membrane between the lobes being festooned. In *L. auricula*, a British species, the membrane is colourless and transparent, the lobes bright red, or green, and the tentacles blue.

As a group the Hydrozoa display regional colouration in a very perfect manner.

II. ACTINOZOA.

It is not necessary to trace the colouration through all the members of this group, but we will trace the variation of colour through two species of anemonies, which have been admirably studied by Dr. A. Andres.* The first column shows the general hue, the second the tints of that hue which are sufficiently marked to form varieties as cochineal red, chocolate, bright red, rufous, liver-coloured, brown, olive, green and glaucous. The third column gives the spotted varieties, from which it will be seen that the chocolate, liver, and green coloured forms have each coloured varieties. It will be seen that the range of colour is very great, passing from pale pink, through yellowish-brown to blue-green.

---

* Fauna und Flora des Golfes von Neapel. Die Actinien. 1884.

Prevailing colour.	Uniform varieties.	Spotted varieties.	Allied species.
White.	?		A. candida.
,,	coccinea.		
,,	chiocca.	tigrina.	
Red.	rubra.		
,,	rufosa.		
Yellow.	hepatica.	fragacea.	
,,	umbra.		
,,	olivacea.		
,,	viridis.	opora.	
,,	glaucus.		
Blue.	?		

Varieties of Actinea Cari.

The following brief descriptions illustrate the distribution of the colour :—

Actinea Cari.

Uniform varieties (*Homochroma*).

	Column.	Tentacles.	Gonidia.	Zone.
α. *Hepatica* ...	red brown.	azure.	azure.	azure.
β. *Rubra* ...	crimson.	violet.		{ wanting, or { flesh coloured.
γ. *Chiocca* ...	scarlet.	white.		
δ. *Coccinea* ...	cochineal.	yellowish.		
ε. *Olivacea* ...	olive-brown green.	azure.	azure.	
ζ. *Viridis* ...	green.	azure.	azure.	azure.

Spotted varieties (*Heterochroma*).

η. *Tigrina* ...	red, spotted yellow			
θ. *Fragacea* ...	liver, spotted clear green.	azure or white.		indistinct.
ι. *Opora* ...	green spotted, and striped yellow	azure.		

In this table the varieties above mentioned are further particularized. The column is the stalk or body, the tentacles are the arms, the gonidia the eye spots, and the zone the line round the base. It will be noticed that these regions are often finely contrasted in colour.

Bunodes gemmaceus is another variable form, and the following varieties are recognised.

Heterochroma.

α. *Ocracea,* (type) } peristome ochre yellow, zone black, tentacles grey, with blue and white spots.

β. *Pallida,* peristome whitish grey unbanded, tentacles with white spots.

γ. *Viridescens,* peristome greenish white unbanded, tentacles with white spots and rosy shades.

δ. *Aurata,* column at base golden, peristome intenser yellow with crimson flush, tentacles grey with ochreous and white spots.

ε. *Carnea,* column at base flesh coloured, peristome rosy, tentacles rosy, with white spots.

Homochroma.

ζ. *Rosea,* like ε, but with rosy tubercles.

η. *Nigricans,* peristome blackish, with blue and green reflexions (*riflessi*).

A few other examples may be given, all of which can be studied in Dr. André's magnificently coloured plates.

Aiptasia mutabilis is yellow brown, the tentacles spotted in longitudinal rows, the spots growing smaller towards the tip, thus affording a perfect example of the adaptation of colour to structure.

Anemonia sulcata has normally long light yellow pendulous tentacles tipped with rose, but a variety has the column still yellow but the tentacles pale green, tipped with rose.

Bunodes rigidus has the column green, with rows of crimson tubercles, the tentacles are flesh-coloured, except the outer row which are pearly ; the peristome is green, with brown lips.

CHAPTER X.

The Colouration of Insects.

IN the decoration of insects and birds, nature has exerted all her power; and amongst the wealth of beauty here displayed we ought to find crucial tests of the views herein advocated. It will be necessary, therefore, to enter somewhat into detail, and we shall take butterflies as our chief illustration, because in them we find the richest display of colouring. The decoration of caterpillars will also be treated at some length, partly because of their beauty, and partly because amongst them sexual selection cannot possibly have had any influence.

Butterflies are so delicate in structure, so fragile in constitution, so directly affected by changes of environment, that upon their wings we have a record of the changes they have experienced, which gives to them a value of the highest character in the study of biology. In them we can study every variation that geographical distribution can effect; for some species, like the Swallow-tail (*Papilio machaon*) and the Painted Lady (*Cynthia cardui*), are almost universal, and others, like our now extinct Large Copper (*Lycæna dispar*), are excessively local, being confined to a very few square miles. From the arctic regions to the tropics, from the mountain tops to the plains, on the arid deserts and amidst luxuriant vegetation, butterflies are everywhere to be found.

Before entering into details, it will be as well to sketch some of the broad features of butterfly decoration. In the first place they are all day-fliers, and light having so strong an influence upon colour, there is a marked difference in beauty between them and the night-flying moths. A collection of butterflies viewed side by side with a collection of moths brings out this fact more strongly than words can describe, especially when the apparent exceptions are considered; for many moths are as brightly coloured as butterflies. These will be found to belong either to day-flying species, like the various Burnets (*Zygæna*), Tiger Moths (*Arctia*), or evening flyers like the Hawk Moths (*Sphyngidæ*.) The true night-flying, darkness-loving moths cannot in any way compare with the insects that delight in sunshine. We see the same thing in birds, for very few nocturnal species, so far as we are aware, are brilliantly decorated.

Another salient feature is the difference that generally exists between the upper and lower surfaces of the wings. As a rule, the upper surface is the seat of the brightest colour. Most butterflies, perhaps all, close their wings when at rest, and the upper wing is generally dropped behind the under wing, so that only the tip is visible. The under surface is very frequently so mottled and coloured as to resemble the insect's natural surroundings, and so afford protection. It does not follow that this protective colouring need be dull, and only when we know the habit of the insect can we pronounce upon the value of such colouring. The pretty Orange-tip has its under wings veined with green, and is most conspicuous in a cabinet, but when at rest upon some umbelliferous plant, with its orange tip hidden, these markings so resemble the environment as to render the insect very inconspicuous. The brilliant *Argynnis Lathonia*, with its underside adorned with plates of metallic silver, is in the cabinet a most vivid and strongly-marked species; but we have watched this insect alight among brown leaves, or on brown stones, outside Florence, where it is very common, and find that these very marks are a sure protection, for the insect at rest is most difficult to see, even when it is marked down to its resting-place.

But some butterflies have parts of the under surface as gaily decorated as the upper; and this not for protection. This may be seen to some extent in our own species, for instance in the orange-tip of the Orange-tip, and the red bar in the upper wing of the Red Admiral (*V. atalanta*). If we watch these insects, the conviction that these are true ornaments is soon forced upon us. The insect alights, perhaps alarmed, closes its wings, and becomes practically invisible. With returning confidence it will gradually open its wings and slowly vibrate them, then close them again, and lift the upper wing to disclose the colour. This it will do many times running, and the effect of the sudden appearance and disappearance of the bright hues is as beautiful as it is convincing. None can doubt the love of display exhibited in such actions.

The delicacy of their organization renders butterflies peculiarly susceptible to any change, and hence they exhibit strong tendencies to variation, which make them most valuable studies. Not only do the individuals vary, but the sexes are often differently coloured. Where two broods occur in a season they are sometimes quite differently decorated, and finally a species inhabiting widely different localities may have local peculiarities.

We can thus study varieties of decoration in many ways, and we shall treat of them as follows:—

1. *Simple Variation*, in which the different individuals of a species vary in the same locality.
2. *Local Variation*, in which the species has marked peculiarities in different localities.
3. *Sexual Dimorphism*, in which the sexes vary.
4. *Seasonal Dimorphism*, in which the successive broods differ.

In order fully to understand the bearing of the following remarks it is necessary to know something of the anatomy and nomenclature of butterflies. Fig. 3 is an ideal butterfly. The wing margins

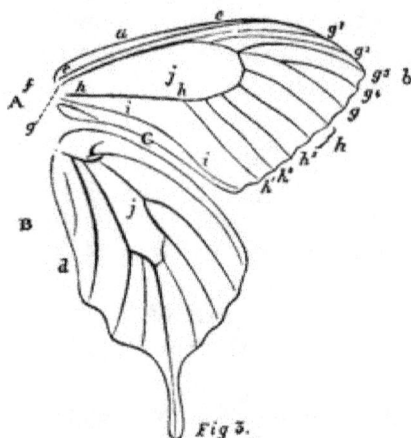

Fig. 3.   Diagram of Butterfly's Wing.

A	Upper Wing.	*f.*	Costal nervure.
B.	Lower Wing.	*g.*	Sub-costal do.
a.	Costal Margin.	g^{1-4}.	Branches of do.
b.	Hind Margin.	*h.*	Median nervure.
c.	Inner „	*i.*	Sub-median do.
d.	Anal Angle.	*j.*	Discoidal Cell.
e.	Costa.	*k.*	Discoidal Veins.

are described as the *Costal*, which is the upper strong edge of the wing, the *Hind* margin, forming the outside, and the *Inner* margin, forming the base. The nervures consist of four principal veins; the *Costal*, a simple nervure under the costa, the *Sub-costal*, which runs parallel to the costal and about halfway to the tip emits branches, generally four in number; the *Median* occupying the centre of the wing and sending off branches, usually three in number, and the *Sub-median* below which is always simple. There are thus two simple nervures, one near the costal the other near the inner margin, and between them are two others which emit branches. Between these two latter is a wide plain space known as the *discoidal cell*. Small veins called the *discoidal* pass from the hind margin towards the cell, and little transverse nervures, known as sub-discoidal, often close the cell. By these nervures the wing is mapped out into a series of spaces of which one, the discoidal cell, is the most important.

The nervures have two functions, they support and strengthen the wing, and being hollow serve to convey nutritive fluid and afterwards air to the wing.

The wings are moved by powerful muscles attached to the base of the wings close to the body and to the inside of the thorax, all the muscles being necessarily internal. "There are two sets which depress the wings; firstly a double dorsal muscle, running longitudinally upwards in the meso-thorax;* and, secondly, the dorso-ventral muscles of the meso and meta-thorax,† which are attached to the articulations of the wings above, and to the inside of the thorax beneath. Between these lie the muscles which raise the wings and which run from the inner side of the back of the thorax to the legs." ‡ When we consider the immense extent of wing as compared with the rest of the body, the small area of attachment, and the great leverage that has to be worked in moving the wings, it is clear that the area of articulation of the wing to the body is one in which the most violent movement takes place. It is here that the waste and repair of tissue must go on with greatest vigour, and we should, on our theory, expect it to be the seat of strong emphasis. Accordingly we commonly find it adorned with hairs, and in a vast number of cases the general hue is darker than that of the rest of the wing, and so far as we have been able to observe, never lighter than the body

* The middle division of the thorax.
† Hinder division of thorax.
‡ Dallas in Cassell's Nat. Hist., vol. vi., p. 27.

of the wing. Even in the so-called whites (Pieris) this part of the wing is dusky, and instances are numerous on Plate IV.

The scales, which give the colour to the wings, deserve more than a passing notice. They are inserted by means of little stalks into corresponding pits in the wing-membrane, and overlap like tiles on a roof; occasionally the attachment is a ball and socket (*Morphinæ*), in which case it is possible the insect has the power of erecting and moving its scales. The shapes are very numerous, but as a rule they are short. To this there is a remarkable exception on the wings of the males of certain butterflies, consisting of elongated tufted prominences which appear to be connected with sense-organs. They are probably scent-glands, and thus we find, even in such minute parts as scales, a difference of function emphasized by difference of ornamentation, here showing itself in variety of forms; but, as we have said, ornamentation in form is often closely allied to ornamentation in colours. In some butterflies, indeed, these scales are aggregated into spots, as in *Danais*, and have a different hue from the surrounding area.

The scales are not simple structures, but consist of two or more plates, which are finely striated. The colouring matter consists of granules, placed in rows between the striæ, and may exist upon the upper surface of the upper membrane (epidermal), or the upper surface of the under or middle plate (hypodermal), or the colour may be simple diffraction colour, arising from the interference of the light-waves by fine striæ.

Dr. Haagen, in the admirable paper before mentioned, has examined this question thoroughly, and gives the results set forth in the following table :—

Epidermal Colours.

Metallic blues and greens	
Bronze	
Gold	
Silver	Persistent after death.
Black	
Brown	
Red (rarely)	

Hypodermal Colours.

Blue
Green
Yellow
Milk-white   } Fading after death.
Orange and
        shades between
Red

The hypodermal colours are usually lighter than the epidermal, and are sometimes changed by a voluntary act. Hypodermal and epidermal colours are, of course, not peculiar to insects; and, as regards the former, it is owing to their presence that the changing hues of fishes, like the sole and plaice, and of the chameleon are due.

The great order Lepidoptera, including butterflies and moths, seems to the non-scientific mind to be composed of members which are pretty much alike, the differences being of slight importance; but this is not in reality the case, for the lepidoptera might, with some accuracy, be compared to the mammalia, with its two divisions of the placental and non-placental animals. Comparing the butterflies (Rhopalocera) to the placental mammals, we may look upon the different families as similar to the orders of the mammalia. Were we as accustomed to notice the differences of butterflies as we are to remark the various forms of familiar animals, we should no longer consider them as slight, but accord to them their true value. When in the mammalia we find animals whose toes differ in number, like the three-toed rhinoceros and the four-toed tapir, we admit the distinction to be great, even apart from other outward forms. So, too, the seal and lion, though both belonging to the carnivora, are readily recognized as distinct, but the seals may easily be confounded by the casual observer with the manatees, which belong to quite a different order.

Thus it is with the Lepidoptera, for from six-legged insects, whose pupæ lie buried beneath the soil, like most moths, we pass to the highest butterflies, whose fore-legs are atrophied, and whose pupæ hang suspended in the open air; and this by easy intermediate stages. Surely, if six-legged mammals were the rule, we should look upon four-legged ones as very distinct; and this is the case with the butterflies. It is necessary to make this clear at starting, in order that we may appreciate to its full value the changes that have taken place in the insects under study.

Butterflies (*Rhopalocera*) are grouped into four sub-families, as under:—

1. *Nymphalidæ,* having the fore-legs rudimentary, and the pupæ suspended from the base of the abdomen.
2. *Erycinidæ,* in which the males only have rudimentary fore-legs.
3. *Lycænidæ,* in which the fore-legs of the males are smaller than those of the females, and terminate in a simple hook.
4. *Papilionidæ,* which have six perfect pairs of legs, and in which the pupæ assume an upright posture, with a cincture round the middle.

It may, at first sight, appear curious that the imperfect-legged *Nymphalidæ* should be placed at the head of the list, but this is based upon sound reasoning. The larva consists of thirteen segments, and, in passing to the mature stage, the second segment alone diminishes in size, and it is to this segment that the first pair of legs is attached. Looking now to the aerial habits of butterflies, we can understand how, in the process of evolution towards perfect aerial structure, the legs, used only for walking, would first become modified; and, naturally, those attached to the segment which decreases with development would be the first affected. When this is found to be combined with an almost aerial position of the pupæ, we see at once how such insects approach nearest to an ideal flying insect. It is a general law that suppression of parts takes place as organisms become specialized. Thus, in the mammalia, the greatest number of toes and teeth are found in the lowest forms and in the oldest, simplest fossil species.

A butterfly is, indeed, little more than a beautiful flying machine; for the expanse of wing, compared with the size of the body, is enormous.

CHAPTER XI.

The Colouration of Insects.

(*Continued.*)

General Scheme of Colouring. So various are the patterns displayed upon the wings of butterflies, that amidst the lines, stripes, bars, dots, spots, ocelli, scalloppings, etc., it seems at first hopeless to detect any general underlying principle of decoration; and this is the opinion that has been, and is still, held by many who have made these insects a special study. Nevertheless, we will try to show that beneath this almost confused complexity lie certain broad principles, or laws, and that these are expressed by the statement that decoration is primarily dependent upon structure, dependent upon the laws of emphasis and repetition, and modified by the necessity for protection or distinction.

To render this subject as plain as possible, British species will be selected, as far as possible, and foreign ones only used when native forms do not suffice.

The body of by far the greater number of species is either darker or of the same tint as the mass of the wings; and only in rare cases lighter. When the body has different tints, it is generally found that the thorax and abdomen differ in colour, and in many cases the base of the thorax is emphasized by a dark or light band.

On the wings the functional importance of the parts attached to the body is generally darker, perhaps never lighter, than the ground of the wing, and is frequently further emphasized by silky hairs. This has already been sufficiently pointed out.

The wing area may be divided into the strong costal margin, the hind margin, the nervules, and the spaces; and, however complex the pattern may be, it is always based upon these structure lines.

M

In the majority of insects the costal margin is marked with strong colour. This may be noticed in *Papilio Machaon, P. merope, Vanessa antiopa,* and the whites in Plate IV. The extreme tip of the fore-wings is nearly always marked with colour, though this may run into the border pattern. This colour is dark or vividly bright, and we know no butterfly, not even dark ones, that has a light tip to the wings. Sometimes, it is true, the light bead-border spots run to the tip, but these are not cases in point. The development of tips has been traced in Chapter VI, and need not be repeated.

The hind margin of both wings is very commonly emphasized by a border, of which *V. Antiopa,* Pl. III. Fig. 3, is a very perfect example.

The border pattern may consist of one or more rows of spots, lines, bands, or scallops;* and there is frequently a fine fringe, which in many cases is white, with black marks, and to which the term bead-pattern may be applied.

A definite relation subsists in most cases between the shape of the hind margin and the character of the border-pattern. The plain or simple bordered wings have plain border patterns, and the scalloped wings have scalloped borders; or rather scalloped borders are almost exclusively confined to scalloped wings. In our English butterflies, for instance, out of the 62 species :—

33 have plain margins to the wings. In all the border is plain, or wanting.

20 have the fore-wings plain, and the hind wings scalloped, and in all the hind-wings are scalloped and the fore-wings plain, or with slightly scalloped border-patterns.

9 have scalloped margins and scalloped border-patterns.

Another relation between structure and pattern is found in those insects which have tailed hind-wings, for the tail is very frequently emphasized by a spot, often of a different colour from the rest of the wing as in the Swallow-Tails, Plates IV. and V.

Yet another point may be noticed. In each wing there is a space, the discoidal cell, *j* Fig. 3, at the apex of which several nervures join, forming knots. These are points at which obstacles exist to the flow of the contents, and they are almost always marked by a distinct pattern. We thus have a discoidal spot in very many butterflies, in

* In the true scallop pattern the convexity is turned towards the body of the insect.

nearly all moths; and in the other orders of winged insects the decoration is even more pronounced, as any one may see who looks at our dragon-flies, wasps, bees, or even beetles.

In some insects the decoration of the body is very marked, as in our small dragon-flies, the Agrions. In one species, for example, *A. Puella*, the male is pale blue banded with black, and the female bronze black, with a blue band on the segment, bearing the sexual organ; the ovipositors are also separately decorated. The male generative organs are peculiar, in that the fertilizing fluid is conveyed from one segment to a reservoir at the other end of the abdomen. Both the segments bearing these organs are marked by special decoration. The peculiar arrangement of the sexual organs in dragon-flies is very variable, and certain segments are modified or suppressed in some forms, as was shown by J. W. Fuller.[*] In every case the decoration follows the modification. In the thorax of dragon-flies, too, the principal muscular bands are marked out in black lines. This distinct representation of the internal structure is beautifully shown in *Æschna* and *Gomphina*, and in the thorax of *Cicada*, as shown by Dr. Haagen in the paper quoted in the last chapter.

We may, then, safely pronounce that the decoration of insects is eminently structural.

Simple Variation. Cases of simple variation have been already cited in our description of spots and stripes, and it only remains to show that in this, as in all other cases, the variation is due to a modification of original structural decoration.

To take familiar examples. Newman, in his British Butterflies, figures the varieties of the very common Small Tortoiseshell (*Vanessa urticæ*). In the normal form there is a conspicuous white spot on the disc of the fore-wings, which is absent in the first variety, owing to the spreading of the red-brown ground colour. This variety is permanent on the Mediterranean shores. In variety two, the second black band, running from the costa across the cell, is continued across the wing. The third variety, Mr. Newman remarks, is "altogether abnormal, the form and colouring being entirely altered." Still, when we examine the insect closely, we find it is only a modification of the original form. The first striking difference is in the margin of the wings, which in the normal form is scalloped with scallop-markings, whereas, in the variety the margins are much simpler, and the border pattern closely corresponds with it, having

---

[*] J. W. Fuller on the Breathing Apparatus of Aquatic Larvæ. Proc. Bristol Nat. Soc.

lost its scalloping. In the fore-wing some of the black bands and spots are suppressed or extended, and the extensions end rigidly at nervules. The dark colouring of the hind-wings has spread over the whole wing. We thus see that the decoration, even in varieties called abnormal, still holds to structural lines, and is a development of pre-existing patterns.

No one can have examined large series of any species without being impressed with the modification of patterns in almost every possible way. For instance, we have reared quantities of *Papilio Machaon*, and find great differences, not only in the pattern, but in the colour itself. A number of pupæ from Wicken Fen, Cambridge-shire, were placed in cages, into which only coloured light could fall, and though these experiments are not sufficiently extended to allow us to form any sound conclusions as to the effect of the coloured light, we got more varieties than could be expected from a batch of pupæ from the same locality. The tone of the yellow, the quantity of red, the proportion of the yellow to the blue scales in the clouds, varied considerably, but always along the known and established lines.

The variations in the colour of Lepidoptera has been most admirably treated by Mr. J. Jenner Weir in a paper, only too short, read before the West Kent Natural History Society.* He divides variations into two sections, Aberrations or Heteromorphism, and constant variations or Orthopæcilism, and subdivides each into six classes, as under :—

Heteromorphism.

Albinism	white varieties.
Melanism	black do.
Xanthism	pallid do.
Sports	or occasional variations not included in the above.
Gynandrochomism ...	females coloured as males.
Hermaphroditism ...	sexes united.

Orthopæcilism.

Polymorphism	variable species.
Topomorphism	local varieties.
Atavism ...	reversion to older forms.
Dimorphism	two constant forms.
Trimorphism... ...	three do. do.
Horeomorphism ...	seasonal variation.

* Entomologist, vol. xvi., p. 169, 1883.

In some cases, he remarks, variations are met with which may with equal propriety be classed in either section.

Albinism he finds to be very rare in British species, the only locality known to him being the Outer Hebrides. This reminds us of Wallace's remark upon the tendency to albinism in islands. Xanthism, he finds to be more plentiful, and quotes the common Small Heath (*Cænonympha pamphilus*) as an illustration. In these varieties we have simply a bleaching of the colouring matter of the wings, and therefore no departure from structural lines. Melanism arises from the spreading of large black spots or bars, or, as in *Biston betularia*, a white moth peppered with black, dots by the confluence of small spots; for this insect in the north is sometimes entirely black. It is singular that insects have a tendency to become melanic in northern and alpine places, and this is especially the case with white or light coloured species. (*See* Plate IV. Fig. 17) It has recently been suggested that this darkening of these delicate membranous beings in cold regions is for the purpose of absorbing heat, and this seems very probable.*

Of ordinary spots it is merely necessary to remark, that they are all cases in our favour. Thus, in *Satyrus hyperanthus* we have "the ordinary round spots . . . changed into lanceolate markings"; this takes place also in *C. davus*. The other cases of aberration do not concern us.

When, however, we come to the cases in which a species has two or more permanent forms, it is necessary to show that they are in all cases founded on structure lines. The patterns, as shown in Plate V., Figs. 1–13, are always arranged structurally, and the fact that not only are intermediate forms known, as in *Araschnia porima*, Plate V., Fig. 6, but that the various forms are convertible into one another, would in itself be sufficient to show that in these cases there is no departure from the general law. In *Grapta interrogationis*, Plate V., Figs. 8–10, we see in the central figure one large spot above the median nervure, in the left-hand form this is surmounted by another spot above the lowest sub-costal branch, and in the right-hand figure this latter spot is very indistinct. We have here a perfect gradation, and the same may be said of the colouration of the lower wings. Take again the three forms of *Papilio Ajax* in the same plate, Figs. 11–13, and we have again only modifications of the same type.

* Nature. R. Meldola on Melanism, 1885.

In local varieties, as in seasonal forms, we have again nothing more than developments of a given type, as is well shown in Plates IV. & V., Figs. 13-18 & 1-13.

When, however, we come to mimetic forms, whether they mimic plants, as in Plate I., or other species, as in Plates II. & III., a difficulty does seem to arise.

The leaf butterfly (*Kallima inachus*), Plate I., offers no trouble when we view the upper surface only with its orange bands, but its under surface, so marvellously like a dead leaf that even holes and microscopic fungi are suggested, does seem very like a case in which structure lines are ignored. Take, for instance, the mark which corresponds to the mid-ribs, running from the tail to the apex of the upper wing; it does not correspond to any structure line of the insect. But if we take allied and even very different species and genera of Indian and Malayan butterflies, we shall find every possible intermediate form between this perfect mimicry and a total lack of such characters. To cite the most recent authority, the various species of the Genera Discophora, Amathusia, Zeuxidia, Thaumantis, Precis, &c., figured so accurately in Distant's Rhopalocera Malayana, will give all the steps.

In the cases of true mimicry, as in Figs. 1-3, Plates II. & III., where insects as different as sheep from cats copy one another, we find that of course structure lines are followed, though the pattern is vastly changed. The *Papilio merope*, Fig. 1, Plate II., which mimics *Danais niavius*, Fig. 3, does so by suppressing the tail appendage, changing the creamy yellow to white — a very easy change, constantly seen in our own Pieridæ — and diffusing the black. A similar case is seen in Figs. 4-5, Plate III., where a normally white butterfly (*Panopœa hirta*) mimics a normally dark one of quite a different section. Here again the change is not beyond our power of explanation. Where a Papilio like *merope* mimics a brown species like *Danais niavius*, we have a still greater change in colour, but not in structural pattern.

If we ascribe to these insects the small dose of intelligence we believe them to possess, we can readily see how the sense of need has developed such forms.

Local varieties present no difficulty under such explanation. The paramount necessity for protection has given the Hebridran species the grey colour of the rocks, and the desert species their sandy hue.

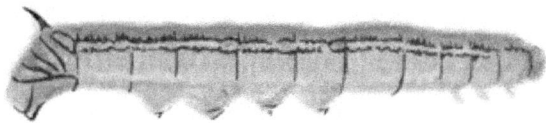

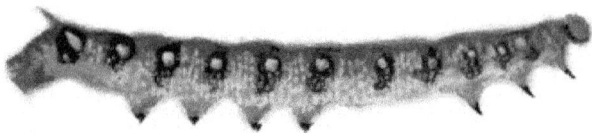

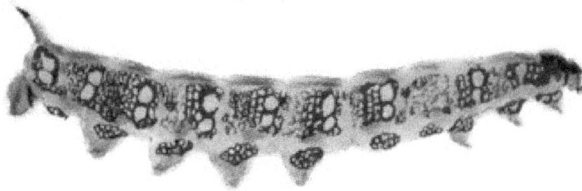

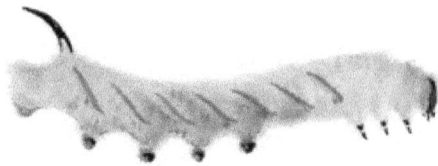

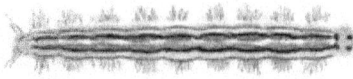

CATERPILLARS.

Finally, to take the case of caterpillars, Weismann has admirably worked out the life history of many forms, and shows how the complex markings have arisen by development. Broadly, a caterpillar consists of 13 segments, the head being one. The head is often marked with darker colour, and the last segment with its clasping feet is also very frequently emphasized, as in Figs. 1 & 3, Plate VII. The spiracles are generally marked by a series of spots, and often connected by a line. Here the tendency to repetition shows itself strongly, for not only the spiracles themselves, but the corresponding points in the segments without spiracles are frequently spotted, and, moreover, these spots are frequently repeated in rows above the spiracular line. Of this, *Deilephila galii* and *D. Euphorbiæ*, Figs. 1-5, Plate VII., are good examples.

The segmentation is also generally emphasized, as shown in all the examples on the plate, but in its simplicity in Fig. 10.

Running down the centre of the back a more or less distinct line is often seen, as shown in the figures. This corresponds with the great dorsal alimentary canal lying just below the skin, and Weismann has shown that in young larvæ this line is transparent, and the green food can be seen through the skin. We have here, perhaps, a relic of the direct colouration noticed in the transparent cœlenterata.

Where larvæ possess horns either upon the head, as in *Apatura iris* and *Papilio machaon*, or on the tail, as in many of the sphyngidæ, like Figs. 1-5, Plate VII., these appendages are always emphasized in colour. As they are frequently oblique, we often find that this obliquity is continued as a slanting spot, as in *D. galii* and *enphorbiæ*, and sometimes repeated as a series of oblique stripes, as in Fig. 4.

It must be admitted that in insects we have strong evidence of structural decoration.

CHAPTER XII.

ARACHNIDA.

THE Arachnida include the scorpions and spiders, and as the former are tolerably uniform in colour, our remarks will be confined to the latter.

The thorax is covered with a horny plate, while the abdomen only possesses a soft skin, and neither show any traces of segmentation. From the thorax spring four pairs of legs, and a pair of palpi, or feelers. Immediately beneath the skin of the abdomen lies the great dorsal vessel, which serves as a heart. This vessel is divided into three chambers, the general aspect of which is shown in Fig. 9, Plate VIII., taken from Gegenbaur's Comparative Anatomy.*

From this heart the blood passes by vessels to each of the limbs, the palpi, etc., as offsets from the double-branched aorta. The shape of this dorsal vessel is peculiar, and its importance in respect to colouration will be immediately apparent.

The primary scheme of colouration in the Arachnida seems to be the distinguishing of the cephalothorax from the abdomen by a different colour. Thus, of the 272 species of British spiders represented in Blackwell's work,† no less than 203 have these parts differently coloured, and only 69 are of the same hue, and even in these there is often a difference of tint. So marked is this in certain cases that the two parts form vivid contrasts. Of this cases are given in the following list.

	Cephalothorax.	Abdomen.
Eresus cinnabarinus,	Black,	Bright Red.
Thomisus floricolens,	Green,	Brown.
——— *cinereus,*	Brown,	Blue.
——— *trux,*	Red,	Brown.
Sparassus smaragdulus,	Green,	Red and yellow.

* Elements of Comparative Anatomy, by C. Gegenbaur. Translated by Jeffrey Bell and Ray Lankester, 1878, p. 285.

† Spiders of Great Britain and Ireland, J. Blackwell. Ray. Soc., 1861.

As a rule the abdomen is darker than the cephalothorax, and many species have the former red-brown and the latter black.

The legs, usually, take the colour of the cephalothorax, and are, hence, generally lighter than the abdomen, but to this there are exceptions. Where the individual legs differ in colour, the two first pairs are the darkest, and the dark hue corresponds in tint with the dark markings on the cephalothorax. The joints of the legs are in many species emphasized with dark colour, which is often repeated in bands along the limb.

The most remarkable point is, however, the pattern on the abdomen, which, though varied in all possible ways, always preserves a general character, so that we might speak with propriety of a spider-back pattern. This pattern is fairly well illustrated in the genus *Lycosa*, but is seen to perfection, and in its simplest form in *Segestria senoculata*, Plate VIII., Fig. 1, and in *Sparassus smaragdulus*, Plate VIII., Fig. 2.

This peculiar pattern is so like the dorsal-vessel that lies just beneath, that it is difficult to avoid the conclusion that we have here an actual case of the influence of internal organs on the integument, and this we believe to be the case. No matter how curious the abdominal markings may seem to be, they never so far depart from this fundamental pattern as to appear independent of it.

Thus, in the genus *Lycosa*, which is by no means the best for the purpose, but is chosen as illustrating Gegenbaur's diagram, Pl. VIII., we have the dorsal-vessel well marked in *L. piscatoria*, Plate VIII., Fig. 3, from which may be developed the other forms. In *L. andrenivora* Plate VIII., Fig. 4, the male shows the vessel-mark attenuated posteriorly; and in the female, Fig. 5, the hinder part has become broken up into detached marks, still preserving the original shape, while the upper part remains practically unchanged. In *L. allodroma* the disintegration of the mark has further advanced, for in the male, Fig. 6, the upper portion has lost something of its shape, and the lower part is a series of isolated segments. This process is carried still further in the female, Fig. 8, where the upper portion is simplified, and the lower almost gone. In *L. campestris*, Fig. 10, the mark is reduced to a stripe, corresponding with the upper part of the vessel-mark only: and, lastly, in the male *L. agretyca*, Fig. 7, this upper part is represented by two spots, though even here traces of the original form can be seen.

A simplification of marking of another sort is seen in *L. rapax,*

Fig. 13, where the chamber-markings are almost obliterated, and merely an irregular stripe left. The stages by which this modification is arrived at are too obvious to need illustration.

In some species the lower portion of the vessel-mark is reduced to small dots, as in *L. cambrica, fluviatilis, piratica,* and others; and the stages are very clear. Starting with the isolated chamber-marks, as in *L. allodroma,* Fig. 5, we get, firstly, a set of spots, as in *L. picta,* which, in the female, Fig. 16, are still connected with the chamber-marks, but in the male, Fig. 17, are isolated. This leads us, by easy steps, to such forms as *L. latitans,* Fig. 14, which consists of a double row of spots upon dark stripes.

The intimate connection thus shown to subsist between the characteristic decoration of the abdomen of spiders, and the shape of the important dorsal organ beneath, seems to be strong evidence of effect that internal structure may have upon external decoration.*

The cephalothorax of spiders, being covered with a hardened membrane, does not show such evidence clearly, for it appears to be a law that the harder the covering tissue, the less does it reflect, as it were, the internal organs. The hard plates of the armadillo are thus in strong contrast to the softer skins of other animals.

Nevertheless, there does appear, occasionally, to be some trace of this kind of decoration in the cephalothorax of certain spiders, though it would be hard to prove. The blood vessels of this part (see Fig. 9). though large, are not nearly so prominent as the great dorsal vessel. The chief artery enters the cephalothorax as a straight tube, forks, and sends branches to the limbs, palpi, and eyes. In many species, notably in the genus *Thomisus,* a furcate mark seems to shadow the forked aorta. This is best shown in *T. luctuosus,* Plate VIII., Fig. 11. Moreover, in this and other genera, lines frequently run to the outer pair of eyes, which alone are supplied with large arteries, see Fig. 9.

However this may be, it is certain that the entire decoration of spiders follows structural lines, and that the great dorsal vessel has been emphasized by the peculiar pattern of the abdomen.

* The decoration of many of the Hoverer flies and wasps is of a similar character

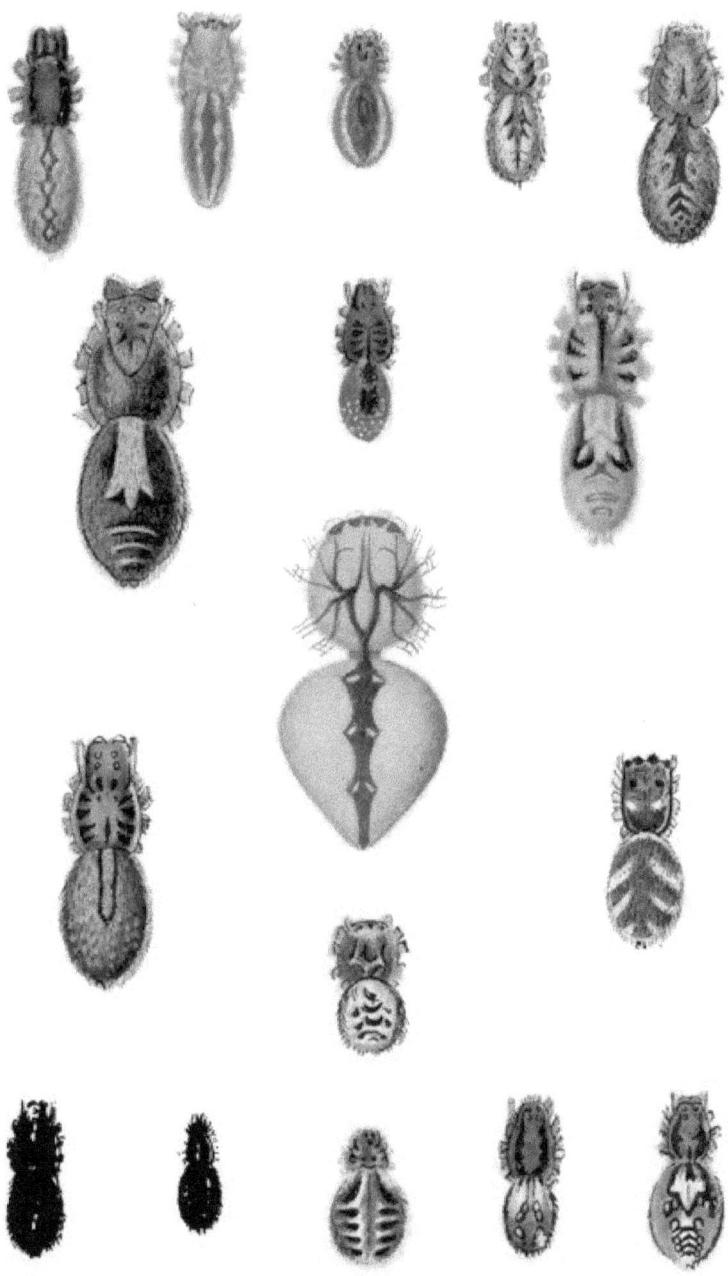

CHAPTER XIII.

COLOURATION OF INVERTEBRATA (*Continued*).

OF the Arthropoda, including the lobsters, crabs, shrimps, etc., little can be said here, as we have not yet been able to study them with anything like completeness. Still, we find the same laws to hold good. The animals are segmented, and we find their system of colouration segmental also. Thus, in the lobsters and crabs there is no dorsal line, but the segments are separately and definitely decorated. The various organs, such as the antennæ and eyes, are picked out in colour, as may be beautifully seen in some prawns.

When we come to the Mollusca, we meet with two distinct types, so far as our subject is concerned; the naked and the shelled. In the naked molluscs, like the slugs, we have decoration applied regionally, as is shown to perfection in the *Nudibranchs*, whose feathery gills are often the seat of some of the most vivid hues in nature.

The shell-bearing mollusca are proverbial for their beauty, but it is essential to bear in mind that the shell does not bear the same relation to the mollusc that the "shell" of a lobster does to that animal. The lobster's shell is part of its living body; it is a true exo-skeleton, whereas the shell of a mollusc is a more extraneous structure—a house built by the creature. We ought, on our view, to find no more relation between the decoration of a shell and the structure of its occupant, than we do in the decoration of a human dwelling-house to the tenant.

The shell consists of carbonate of lime, under one or both of the forms known to mineralogists as calcite and aragonite. This mineral matter is secreted by an organ called the mantle, and the edge, or lip, of the mantle is the part applied to this purpose. The edge of the mantle is the builder's hand, which lays the calcareous stones of the edifice. The shell is built up from the edge, and the action is not continuous but seasonal, hence arise the markings known as lines of growth. In some cases the mantle is expanded at times into wing-like processes, which are turned back over the shell, and deposit additional layers, thus thickening the shell.

In all the forms of life hitherto considered the colouring matter is deposited, or formed, in the substance of the organ, or epidermal covering, but in the mollusca this is not the case. The colouring matter is entirely upon the surface, and is, as it were, stencilled on to the colourless shell. This is precisely analogous to the colouring of the shells of birds' eggs. They, too, are calcareous envelopes, and the colouring matter is applied to the outside, as anyone can see by rubbing a coloured egg. In some eggs several layers of colouring matter are superimposed.

In no case does the external decoration of molluscan shells follow the structure lines of the animal, but it does follow the shape of the mantle. The secreting edge may be smooth, as in *Mactra*, regularly puckered, as in most *Pectens*, puckered at certain points, as in *Trigonia*, or thrown into long folds, as in *Spondylus*. In each of these cases the shell naturally takes the form of the mantle. It is smooth in *Mactra*, regularly ribbed in *Pecten*, tubercled in *Trigonia*, and spined in *Spondylus*. Where the inside of the shell is coloured as in some Pectens, regional decoration at once appears and the paleal lines, and muscular impressions are bounded or mapped out with colour.

It is a significant fact that smooth bivalves are not so ornate as rugose ones, and that the ridges, spines, and tubercles of the latter are the seats of the most prominent colour.

Similar remarks apply to univalve shells, which are wound on an imaginary vertical axis. They may be smooth, as in *Conus* and *Oliva*, rugose, as in *Cerithium*, or spined, as in *Murex*. The structure of these shells being more complex than that of bivalves, we find, as a rule, they are more lavishly ornamented, and the prominent parts of the shell, and especially the borders, are the seat of strongest colour. In some cases, as in adult Cowries (*Cypræa*), the mantle is reflexed so as to meet along the median line, where we see the darkest colour.

The rule amongst spiral shells is to possess spiral and marginal decoration, and this is what we should expect. The Nautilus repeats in the red-brown markings of its shell, the shape of the septa which divide the chambers, though, as is often the case, they are generally more numerous than the septa.

The naked Cephalopoda, or cuttle-fishes, often possess a distinct dorsal stripe, and when our views were first brought before the Zoological Society, this fact was cited as an objection. To us it seems one of the strongest of favourable cases, for these animals possess a sort of backbone—the well-known cuttle-bone—and hence they have a dorsal line.

Some shells, as *Margarita catenata*, have a chain-pattern, and in this case the action of the pigment cells takes place at regular and short intervals. Others, as *Mactra stultorum*, the stencilling forms a series of lines and spots, generally enlarging into rays.

The whole subject of the decoration of shells deserves much more time than we have been able to give to it as yet.

CHAPTER XIV.

COLOURATION OF VERTEBRATA.

THE vertebrata, as their name implies, are distinguished by the possession of an internal skeleton, of which the backbone is the most essential part, and the general, but not universal, possession of limbs or appendages.

Consequently we find that the dorsal and ventral surfaces are almost invariably coloured differently, and the dorsal is the darker in the great majority of instances. Generally the spine is marked by a more or less defined central line, and hence this system of colouration may be termed axial, because it is in the direction of the axes, or applied about the axes.

Fishes. Where fishes have not been modified out of their original form, as are the soles, plaice, and other flat fish, we find the dorsal region darker than the ventral, and even here the under surfaces are the lightest. Even in cases like the Char, Fig. 1, Plate IX., where vivid colour is applied to the abdomen, the dorsum is the darker. The dorsum is often marked by a more or less well-defined dark band, as in the mackerel and perch, Fig. 2, Plate IX. There are sometimes parallel bands at right angles to the above, as in the perch and mackerel; and this is a common feature, and apparently a very old one, as we find it in the young of fishes whose adults are without these rib-like marks, such as the trout and pike.

It is only necessary to inspect any drawings of fishes to see that their colouration is on a definite principle, although rather erratic. Important functional parts, like the gills, fins, and tail, are generally marked in colour more or less distinctly, as may be seen, for instance, in our common fresh-water fishes, like the roach and perch. The line of mucus-secreting glands running along the sides is usually

marked by a dark line. These facts point distinctly to structural decoration.

There are in some fishes, like the John Dory, curious eye-like dark spots, which we cannot refer to a structural origin, though a better acquaintance with the class might reveal such significance.

The Amphibia have not been well studied by us, and we must leave them with the remark that they seem to bear out the view of structural decoration, as is seen in our English newts. Some are, however, modified out of all easy recognition.

Reptiles. Among the reptiles, the snakes, Fig. 4, may be selected for illustration. Snakes are practically little more than elongated backbones, and are peculiar from the absence of limbs. The colouring matter does not reside so much in the scales as in the skin beneath, so that the sloughs do not illustrate the decoration. Hence, we might expect to find here a direct effect of morphological emphasis.

The ornamentation of snakes is very similar throughout the class, both in water and land snakes; as may be seen by Sir W. Fayrer's work on Venomous Snakes. This ornamentation is of a vertebral pattern, placed along the dorsal surface, with cross lines, which may represent ribs.

Where the ribs are wanting, as in the neck, the pattern changes, and we get merely longitudinal markings.

In the Python, Fig. 4, there are, near the central line, numerous round spots, which apparently emphasize the neural processes. There are diagonal markings on some species which illustrate the development of colour-spots already alluded to.

This snake-pattern is very singular and striking. The markings are fewer in number than the vertebræ, yet their true vertebral character is most obvious.

In Snakes, again, we find the dorsal region is darker than the ventral.

In the Lizards there are patches of colour placed axially, while each patch covers a number of scales.

Birds. Birds have their whole economy modified to subserve their great functional peculiarity of flight.

Immense muscles are required for the downward stroke of the wing, and to give attachment to these the sterum has a strongly developed keel. To bring the centre of gravity low, even the muscles which raise the wing are attached to the sternum, or breast-

bone, instead of to the dorsal region, as might be expected; and to
brace the wings back a strong furculum—the merry-thought—is
attached. The breast, then, is the seat of the greatest functional
activity in birds, and, consequently, we find in a vast number of
birds that the breast is the seat of vivid colour.

As many birds are modified for protective purposes, the brightest
species were selected to test our views, namely, the Birds of
Paradise (Paradisea), Humming Birds (Trochilidæ), and Sun Birds
(Nectarinidæ). In these birds it is clear that colour has had full
sway, untramelled by any necessity for modification.

Nothing is more striking than the mapping out of the surface of
these birds into regions of colour, and these regions are always
bounded by structural lines.

Take, for instance, *Paradisea regia.* In this bird we find the
following regions mapped in colour:—

Sternum	... ...	brown.
Clavicle	... ...	yellow.
Pelvis	... ...	yellow.
Band	... ...	brown.
Frontal bone	... ...	black.
Parutal bones	... ...	green.
Occiput	... ...	yellow.

A beautiful ruff emphasizes the pectoral muscles, and the tail
appendages emphasize the share-like caudal vertebræ.

If we turn to the other species of this genus, we find in *P. Papuana*
the claret breast suddenly change to green at the furculum; and
similar changes take place in *P. speciosa,* while in *P. Wallacri* and
Wilsoni this region is decorated with a wonderful apron of metallic
green.

The region of the furculum is equally well marked in the Toucans
and Sun-birds.

If now we observe the back of a bird, and view the skeleton with
the wings at rest, we shall find it falls into three morphological
tracts. First, the shoulder, or scapular track; second, the thigh, or
pelvic; third, the tail, or caudal region; and in all these birds the
several tracts are beautifully marked by sudden and contrasted
change of colour. In *P. Wilsoni* all the tracts are brilliant red, but
they are separated by jet-black borders. In *Nectarinea chloropygia*
the scapular region is red, the pelvic yellow, and the caudal green.

1

2

- E Swert-hiv del   SUN BIRDS.

In *P. Wilsoni* we have a wonderful example of morphological emphasis. The head is bare of feathers, and coloured blue, except along the sutures of the skull, where lines of tiny black feathers map out the various bones.

But morphological emphasis exists everywhere in birds. The wing-primaries, which attach to the hand, are frequently differently decorated from the secondaries, which feathers spring from the ulna; and the spur-feathers of the thumb, or pollux, are different in shape, and often in colour, from the others, as every fly-fisher who has used woodcock spur-feathers knows full well. The wing-coverts and tail-coverts are frequently mapped in colour; and the brain case is marked by coloured crests. The eye and ear are marked by lines and stripes; and so we might go on throughout the whole bird. We may remark that these very tracts are most valuable for the description and detection of species, and among ornithologists receive special names.

Now, this distribution of colour is the more remarkable inasmuch as the feathers which cover the surface—the contour feathers—are not evenly distributed over the body, but are confined to certain limited tracts, as shown by Nitzsch; and though these tracts have a morphological origin, they are rendered quite subsidiary to the colouration, which affects the whole bird, and not these regions in particular. In fact, the colouration is dependent upon the regions on which the feathers lie, and not upon the area from which they spring. In other words, we seem to have in birds evidence of the direct action of underlying parts upon the surface.

In more obscurely coloured birds, and those which seem to be evenly spotted, close examination shows that even here the decoration is not uniform, but the sizes and axes of the spots change slightly as they occupy different regions; as may be seen in Woodpeckers and Guinea-fowl.

Although the same tone of colour may prevail throughout the plumage, as in the Argus Pheasant, great variety is obtained by the fusion of spots into stripes. A symmetrical effect is produced by the grouping of unsymmetrical feathers; as is so often seen in plants, where irregular branches and leaves produce a regular contour.

Sometimes, especially on the breast and back, the feathers of one region seem to unite so as to form one tract, so far as colour is concerned. Thus, if in *P. Wilsoni* the black borders of the dorsal regions were suppressed, all three areas would be of one hue. This seems to have been the case in the breast region of Humming Birds, where only the throat is highly coloured. In the Toucans the breast and throat regions are often marked with colour; but sometimes the hue is the same and the boundaries of the regions marked with a band of another colour; if this boundary band be increased, the regions do not seem so well shown, for the boundary becomes as broad as the area; yet, in all these cases the dependence upon regional decoration is manifest. No doubt the few uniformly coloured birds were derived from species which were once variously hued; the gradation of colour being lost in transmission.

Mammalia. The axial decoration of the mammalia is very definite, and nearly all species have a dorsal tract marked with colour. The dark bands on the back of the horse, ox, and ass, are cases in point. In nearly every case the dorsal is darker than the ventral surface.

If we take highly decorated species, that is, animals marked by alternate dark and light bands, or spots, such as the zebra, some deer, or the carnivora, we find, first, that the region of the spinal column is marked by a dark stripe (Figs. 9 & 16); secondly, that the regions of the appendages, or limbs, are differently marked; thirdly, that the flanks are striped, or spotted, along or between the regions of the lines of the ribs; fourthly, that the shoulder and hip regions are marked by curved lines; fifthly, that the pattern changes, and the direction of the lines, or spots, at the head, neck, and every joint of the limbs; and lastly, that the tips of the ears, nose, tail, and feet, and the eye are emphasized in colour. In spotted animals the greatest length of the spot is generally in the direction of the largest development of the skeleton.

This morphological arrangement can be traced even when the decoration has been modified. Thus, in the carnivora we have the lion and puma, which live in open country, with plain skins, the tiger with stripes, an inhabitant of the jungle, and the leopard, ocelot, and jaguar with spots, inhabiting the forests.

But the lion has a dark dorsal stripe, and the nose, etc., are emphasized in colour, and, moreover, the lion has probably lost its marked decoration for protective purposes, for young lions are spotted. The tiger's stripes start from the vertebrae, and still follow the lines of the ribs. In the tiger the decoration changes at the neck, and on the head, and the cervical vertebrae are often indicated by seven stripes. See Fig. 5.

The markings over the vertebræ are not in continuous lines, as in many mammals, but form a series of vertebra-like spots. This plan of decoration is continued even on the tail, which is coloured more on the upper than on the lower surface.

The spotted cats have their spot-groups arranged on the flanks in the direction of the ribs, at the shoulder and haunch in curves, at the neck in another pattern, on the back of the head in another; and the pattern changes as each limb-joint is reached, the spots decreasing in size as the distance is greater from the spine. See Figs. 9-15.

There is in tigers, and the cat-tribe generally, a dark stripe over the dental nerve ; and the zygoma, or cheek-bone, is often marked by colour. Even the supraorbital nerve is shown in the forehead, and there are dark rings round the ears. In dissecting an ocelot at the Zoological Gardens in 1883, a forked line was found immediately over the fork of the jugular vein.

The colouration in these animals seems often to be determined by the great nerves and nerve-centres, and the change from spots, or stripes, to wrinkled lines on the head are strikingly suggestive of the convolutions of the brain, falling. as they do, into two lateral masses, corresponding with the cerebral hemispheres, separated by a straight line, corresponding with the median fissure. This is well shown in the ocelot, Fig. 15, and in many other cats.

That the nerves can affect the skin has already been pointed out in Chapter VI., in the case of herpes, and that it can affect colour is shown in the Hindoo described in the same place.

So marked, indeed, is this emphasis of sensitive parts that every hair of the movable feelers of a cat is shown by colour to be different in function from the hairs of the neck, or from the stationary mass of hair from which the single longer hair starts.

In the Badger, Fig. 16, there is a bulge-shaped mass of coloured hair near the dorsal and lumbar regions, but it is axially placed. The shoulder and loins are well marked, although in a different manner from other species. In some species of deer, and other mammalia, there are white or coloured lines parallel to the spine, and also, as in birds, spots coalesce and form lines, and lines break up into spots.

The great anteater has what at first seems an exceptional marking on the shoulder, but a careful examination of the fine specimen which died at the Zoological Gardens in 1883, we were struck with the abnormal character of the scapula, and we must remember that, as Wallace and Darwin have pointed out, all abnormal changes of the teeth are correlated with changes in the hair. Moreover the muscles of the shoulder region are so enormously developed as to render this otherwise defenceless animal so formidable that even the jaguar avoids an embrace which tightens to a death-grip. This region is, therefore, precisely the one we should expect to be strongly emphasized. This being the case, we have really no exception in this creature.

Certain mammals are banded horizontally along their sides, thus losing most of their axial decoration, and this is well shown among the Viverridæ, and smaller rodents. Now, however conspicuous such animals may appear in collections, they are in their native haunts very difficult to detect. In all cases there is a marked dorsal line; and we suggest that the mature decoration is due to a suppression of the axial decoration for protective purposes, and a repetition of the dorsal decoration according to the law before enunciated. Indeed, in one case we were able to trace this pretty clearly, in the beautiful series of *Sus vittatus* in the museum at Leyden. This pig, an inhabitant of Java, when mature is a dark brown animal, but in the very young state it is clearly marked in yellow and brown, with a dark dorsal stripe, and spots, taking the line of the ribs, and over the shoulder and thigh. As the animal grows older, the spots run into stripes, and it becomes as clearly banded horizontally as the viverridæ. Finally the dark bands increase in width, until they unite, and the creature becomes almost uniformly brown.

We have not been able to see young specimens of the viverridæ, but a similar change may there occur, or it may have occurred in former times. We must also remember that these creatures are long-bodied, like the weasels, and hence they may have a tendency to produce long stripes.

In the case of our domestic animals, especially the oxen, the decoration seems often to have become irregular, but even here the emphasis of the extremities is generally clearly made out, and that of the limbs can often be traced. In horses this is better shown, and dappled varieties often well illustrate the points. Most horses at some time show traces of spots.

Sufficient has now been said to point out the laws we believe to have regulated the decoration of the animal kingdom. The full working out of the question must be left to the future, but it is hoped that a solid groundwork has been laid down.

LEAVES

CHAPTER XV.

THE COLOURATION OF PLANTS.

THE general structure of plants is so simple in comparison with that of animals that our remarks upon this sub-kingdom need only be short.

With regard to leaves, especially such as are brightly coloured, like the Begonias, Caladimus, Coleus, and Ancechtochilus, Plate XI., the colour follows pretty closely the lines of structure. We have border decoration, marking out the vein-pattern of the border; the veins are frequently the seat of vivid colour, and when decolouration takes place, as in variegated plants, we find it running along the interspaces of the veins. These facts are too patent to need much illustration; for our zonale geraniums, ribbon grasses, and beautiful-leaved plants generally, are now so common that everyone knows their character. When decay sets in, and oxidation gives rise to the vivid hues of autumn, we find the tints taking structural lines, as is well shown in dying vine and horse-chestnut leaves, Fig. 1, Plate XI. This shows us that there is a structural possibility of acquiring regional colouration.

We must remember, too, that the negative colouration of these dying leaves is of very much the same character as the positive colouration of flowers, for flowers are modified leaves, and their hues are due to the oxidation of the valuable chlorophyll.

In leaves the tendency of spots to elongate in the direction of the leaf is very marked, as may be well seen in Begonia. Fig. 17, drawn to illustrate another point, shows this partly. When leaves are unsymmetrical, like the begonias, the pattern is unsymmetrical also.

Among parallel veined leaves we find parallel decoration. Thus, in the *Calatheas* we have dark marks running along the veins. In *Dracæna ferrea* we have a dark green leaf, with a red border and tip, the red running downwards along the veins. This action may be continued until the leaf is all red except the mid-rib, which remains green. In long net-veined leaves we may cite *Pavetta Borbonica*, whose dark green blade has a crimson mid-rib. Of unsymmetrical leaves those in the plate may suffice.

When we come to flowers, the same general law prevails, and is generally more marked in wild than in cultivated forms, which have been much, and to some extent unnaturally, modified. Broadly speaking, when a flower is regular the decoration is alike on all the parts ; the petals are alike in size, the decoration is similar in each, but where they differ in size the decoration changes. Thus, in *Pelargoniums* we may find all five petals alike, or the two upper petals may be longer or shorter than the lower three. In the first case each is coloured similarly, in the other the colour pattern varies with the size of the petal. The same may be seen in Rhododendron.

Where the petals are united the same law holds good. In regular flowers, like the lilies, the colouration is equal. In irregular flowers, like the snapdragon and foxglove, the decoration is irregular. In Gloxinia the petals may be either regular or irregular, and the decoration changes in concert.

A very instructive case was noticed by one of us in *Lamium galeobdolon*, or yellow Archangel. This plant is normally a labiate with the usual irregular corolla, but we have found it regular, and in this instance the normal irregular decoration was changed to a regular pattern on each petal.

In gamopetalous flowers the line of junction of the petals is frequently marked with colour, and we know of no case in which a pattern runs deliberately across this structure line, though a blotch may spread from it.

When we remember that flowers are absolutely the result of the efforts of plants to secure the fertilizing attention of insects, and that they are supreme efforts, put forth at the expense of a great deal of vegetable energy—that they are sacrifices to the necessity for offspring—it does strike us forcibly when we see that even under these circumstances the great law of structural decoration has to be adhered to.

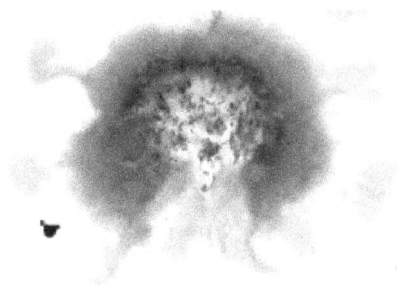

1

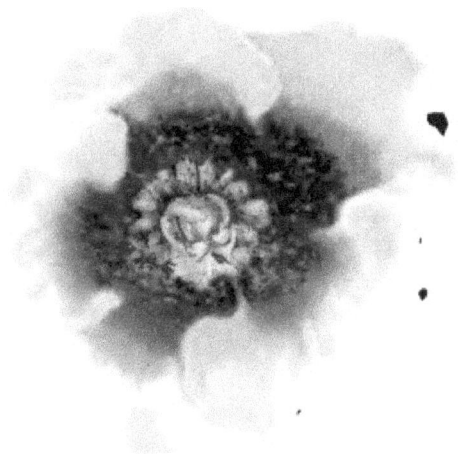

2

3

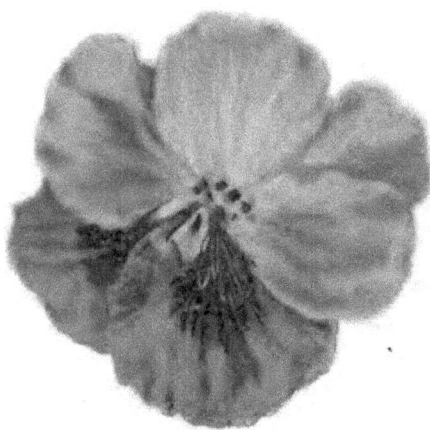

4

CHAPTER XVI.

CONCLUSIONS.

WE have now, more or less fully, examined into the system of colouration in the living world, and have drawn certain inferences from the facts observed.

It appears that colouration began—perhaps as a product of digestion—by the application of pigment to the organs of transparent creatures. Supposing that evolution be true—and, if we may not accept this theory there is no use in induction whatever—it must follow that even the highest animals have in the past been transparent objects. This was admirably illustrated by Prof. Ray Lankester in a lecture on the development of the eyes of certain animals, before the British Association meeting at Sheffield, in which it was shown that the eyes commenced below the surface, and were useful even then, for its "body was full of light."

Granting this, it follows that the fundamental law of decoration is a structural one. Assuming, as we do, that memory has played a most important part in evolution, it follows that all living matter has a profound experience in decorating its organs—it is knowledge just as anciently acquired, and as perfectly, as the power of digestion. This colour was produced under the influence of light—so it is even in opaque animals.

With a knowledge so far reaching, we might expect that even in opaque animals the colouring would still follow structural lines, and there should still be traces of this, more or less distinct.

This is precisely what we do find; and, moreover, we sometimes get a very fair drawing of the important hidden parts, even where least expected, as in a cat's head, a snake's body, a dragon-fly's thorax, a spider's abdomen, a bird's skull.

But if animals thus learned to paint themselves in definite patterns, we might expect that when called upon to decorate *for the sake of beauty* certain parts not structurally emphatic, they would adopt well-known patterns, and hence arose the law of repetition.

But with wider experience came greater powers, and the necessity for protection arising, the well-known patterns were enlarged, till an uniform tint is produced, as in the Java pig, or some repeated at the expense of others, as in the civets. But so ingrained is the tendency to structural decoration that even where modification has reached its highest level, as in the leaf-butterflies, some trace of the plan that the new pattern was founded on is recognisable, just as the rectangular basis can be traced in the arabesque ornaments of the Alhambra.

The pointing out of this great fact has seemed to us a useful addition to the great law of evolution. It supplements it; it gives a reason why.

Could he who first saw these points have read these final pages, it would have lightened the responsibility of the one upon whom the completion of the work has fallen. But he died when the work was nearly finished. The investigation is of necessity incomplete, but nothing bears such misstatements as truth, and though specialists may demur to certain points, the fundamental arguments will probably remain intact.

FINIS

GLOSSARY.

ACETABULA. Lat. *acetabulum*, a little vessel. Sucking discs as on the tentacles of *Physalia*.

AORTA. Gr. The chief artery.

CEPHALOTHORAX. Gr. *kephale*, head; *thorax*, chest. The anterior division of the body in Crustacea and Arachnida, composed of the amalgamated segments of the head and thorax.

CILIA. Lat. *cilium*, an eyelash. Microscopic filaments having the power of vibratory movement.

CŒNOSARC. Gr. *Koinos*, common; *sarx*, flesh. The common stem uniting the separate animals of compound hydrozoa, &c.

CORPUSCLE. Lat. *corpusculum*, a little body. Small coloured bodies, as in the endoderm of hydra, p. 59.

DIFFERENTIATED. Modified into definite organs, or parts; as distinct from structureless protoplasm.

ECTODERM. Gr. *ektos*, outside, *derma*, skin. The internal layer or skin of the Cœlenterata.

EFFERENT. Lat. *effero*, to carry out. A vessel which carries fluids out of the body is said to be efferent.

ENDODERM. Gr. *endon*, within, *derma*, skin. The inner layer or skin of Cœlenterata. *See* ECTODERM.

ENDOSARC. Gr. *endon*, within, *sarx*, flesh. The inner layer of sponges.

EPIDERMAL. Gr. *epi*, upon; *derma*, skin. Relating to the outer layer of skin. As applied to colour, surface pigment as distinct from hypodermal, or deep-seated colour.

GASTROVASCULAR CANAL. Gr. *gaster*, belly, Lat. *vasculum*, a little vessel. The canals or vessels in the umbrella (*manubrium*) of hydrozoa.

GONIDIA. Gr. *gonos*, offspring; *oidos*, like. Reproductive bodies in Sea-anemones.

HYDRANTH. Gr. *hudor*, water; *anthos*, flower. The bodies or polypes of hydroids which exercise nutritive functions. They were called polypites by Huxley.

HYDROPHYLLIA. Gr. *hudor* and *phyllon*, a leaf. Leaf-like organs protecting the polypites of hydrozoa.

HYDROSOMA. Gr. *hudor* and *soma*, body. The entire organism of a hydrozöon.

HYPODERMAL. Gr. *hypo*, beneath; *derma*, skin. In colour, such as lies beneath the surface, as distinct from epidermal.

P

LYTHOCYSTS. Gr. *lythos*, stone, *kystis*, a bladder. Sense organs in hydroids, consisting of transparent capsules inclosing round transparent concretions.

MANUBRIUM. Lat. a handle. The central polypite suspended from the interior of the umbrella of hydroids.

MESODERM. Gr. *mesos*, intermediate; *derma*, skin. The middle layer of sponges, &c.

MESOTHORAX. Gr. *mesos* and *thorax*. The middle division of the thorax in insects, carrying the second pair of legs.

PERISTOME. Gr. *peri*, about; *stoma*, a mouth. The area surrounding the mouth in sea-anemones.

PNEUMATOCYST. Gr. *pneuma*, air; *kystis* a bladder. The air-sac contained in the pneumatophore, see below.

PNEUMATOPHORE. Gr. *pneuma*; *phero*, to carry. The float of certain hydrozoa (*Physophoridæ*.)

POLYPITE. Gr. *polus*, many; *pous*, foot. The separate animal or zöoid of a hydrozöon. *See* HYDRANTH.

PROTOPLASM. Gr. *protos*, first; *plasso*, I mould. The jelly-like matter which forms the basis of all tissues. It is identical with the *sarcode* or flesh of protozoa.

SAC. Lat. *saccus*, a bag, a small cell.

SARCODE. Gr. *sarx*, flesh; *eidos*, form. The protoplasm of protozoa, &c., which see.

SPADIX. Lat. *spadix*, a broken palm branch. In zoology a hollow process occupying the axis of the generative buds of hydrozoa.

SPOROSAC. Gr. *spora*, a seed, and *sac*. The body containing the ova of hydrozoa.

SOMATIC FLUID. Gr. *soma*, the body. The fluid which contains digested food, and taking the place of blood, circulates through the body of hydrozoa.

TENTACLES. Lat. *tentaculus*, a little arm. The arms or prehensile organs of Sea-anemones, &c.

THREAD CELLS. Cells containing an extensible microscopic thread, possessing stinging properties, common among the *Cœlenterata*.

THORAX. Gr. a breastplate. The chest.

INDEX.

Fig. 4.—PYTHON.

Showing vertebra-like markings.

Q

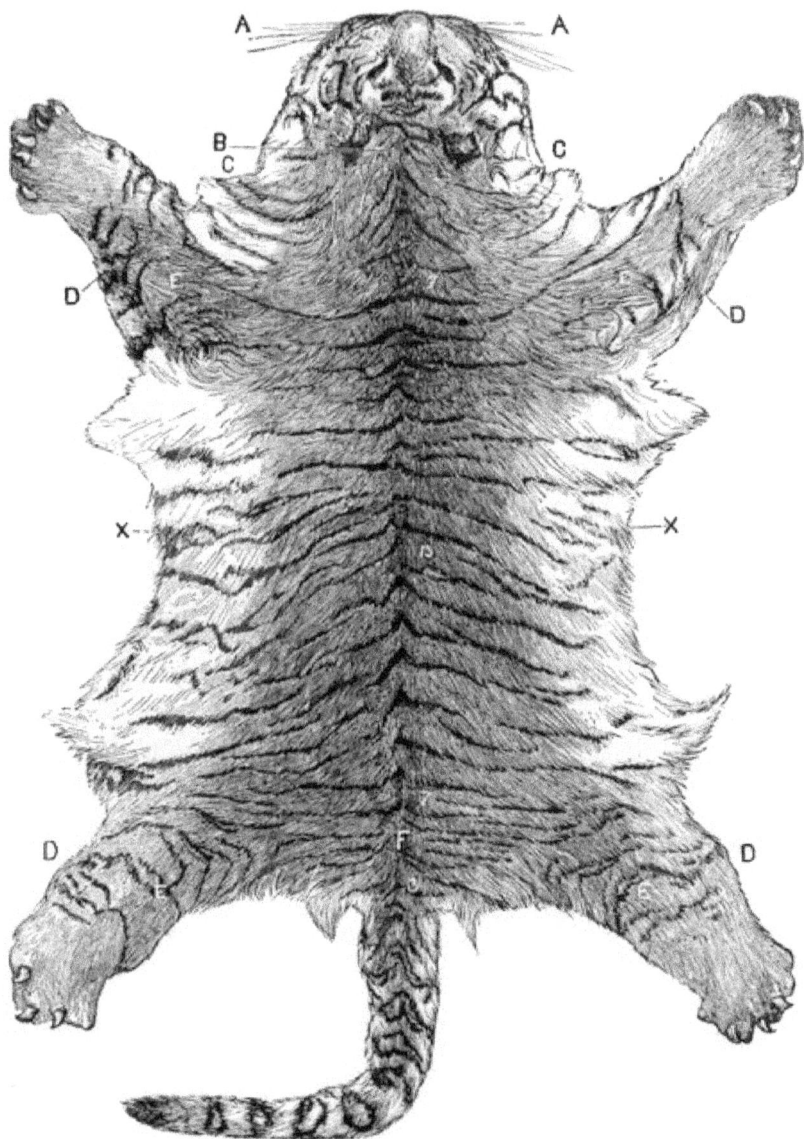

Fig. 5.—TIGER.

The pattern changes at the points lettered.

Q²

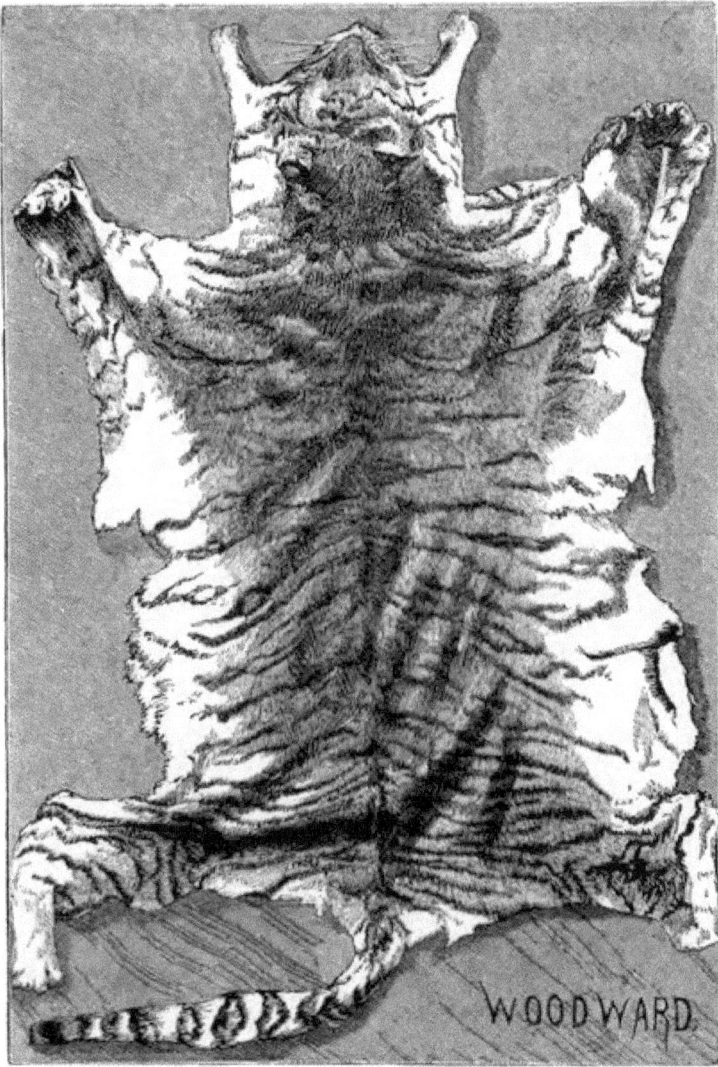

Fig. 6.—TIGER.

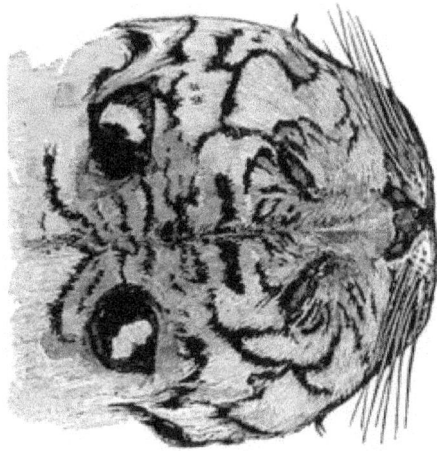

Fig. 8.—Tiger.

*Showing cerebral markings, and markings
over nerves near the eyes.*

Fig. 7.—Tiger.

Showing supra-orbital nerve mark.

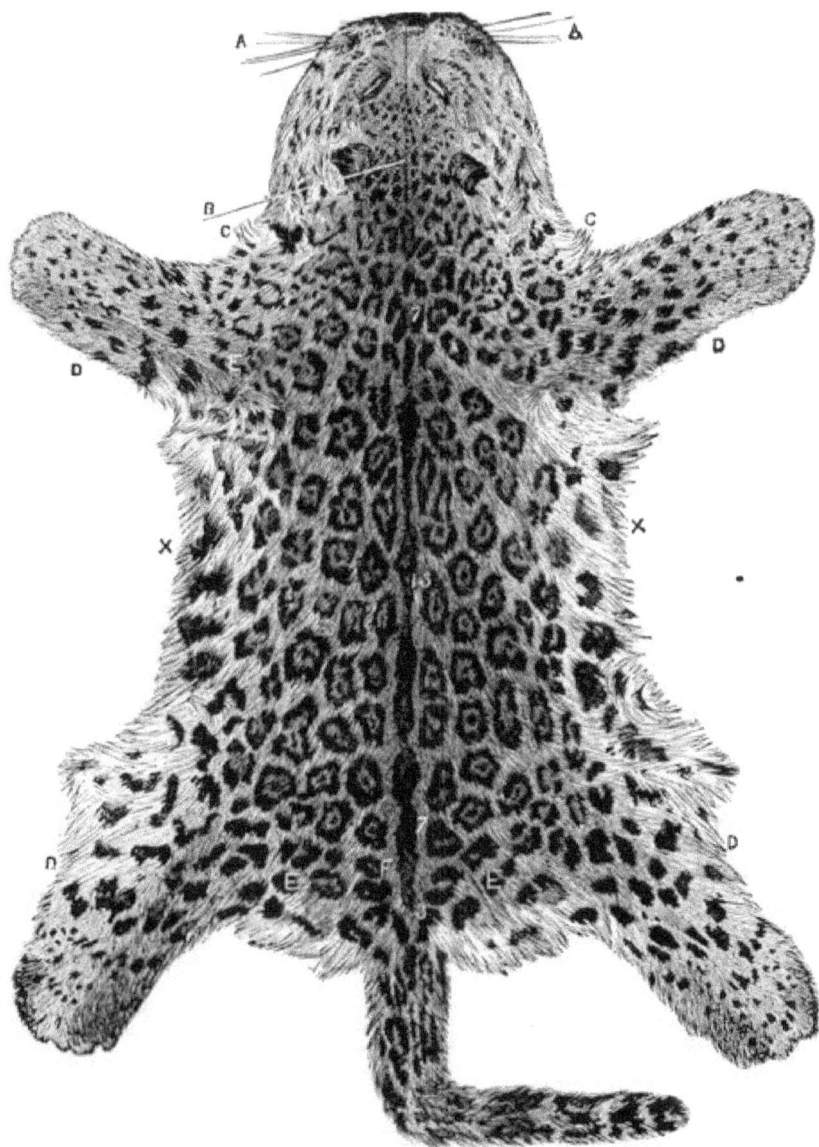

Fig. 9.—LEOPARD.

The pattern changes at the points lettered.

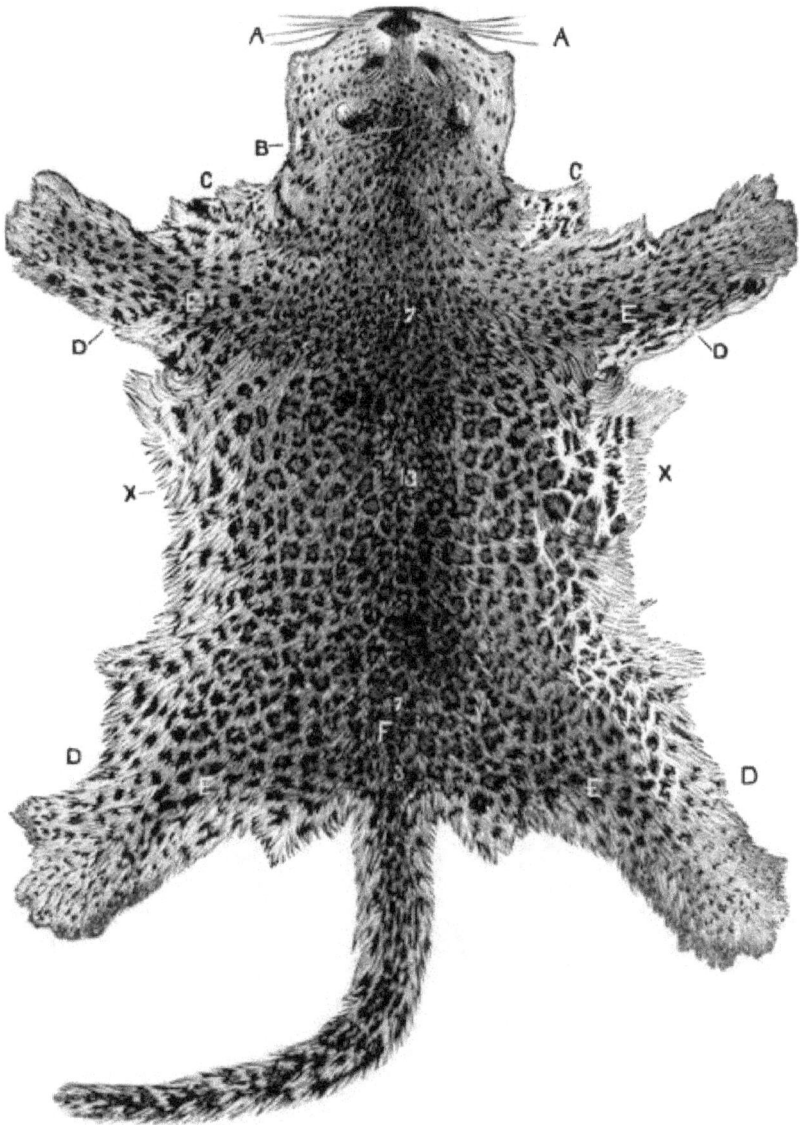

Fig. 10.—LEOPARD.

The pattern changes at the points lettered.

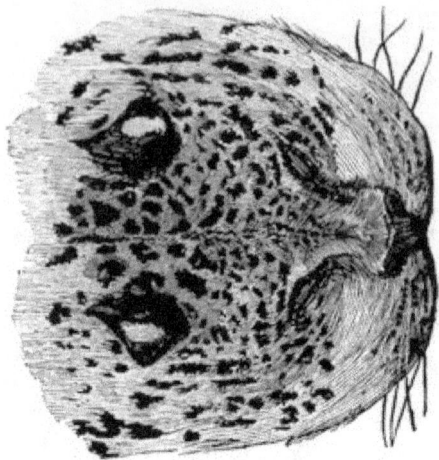

Figs. 11, 12.—LEOPARDS' HEADS.

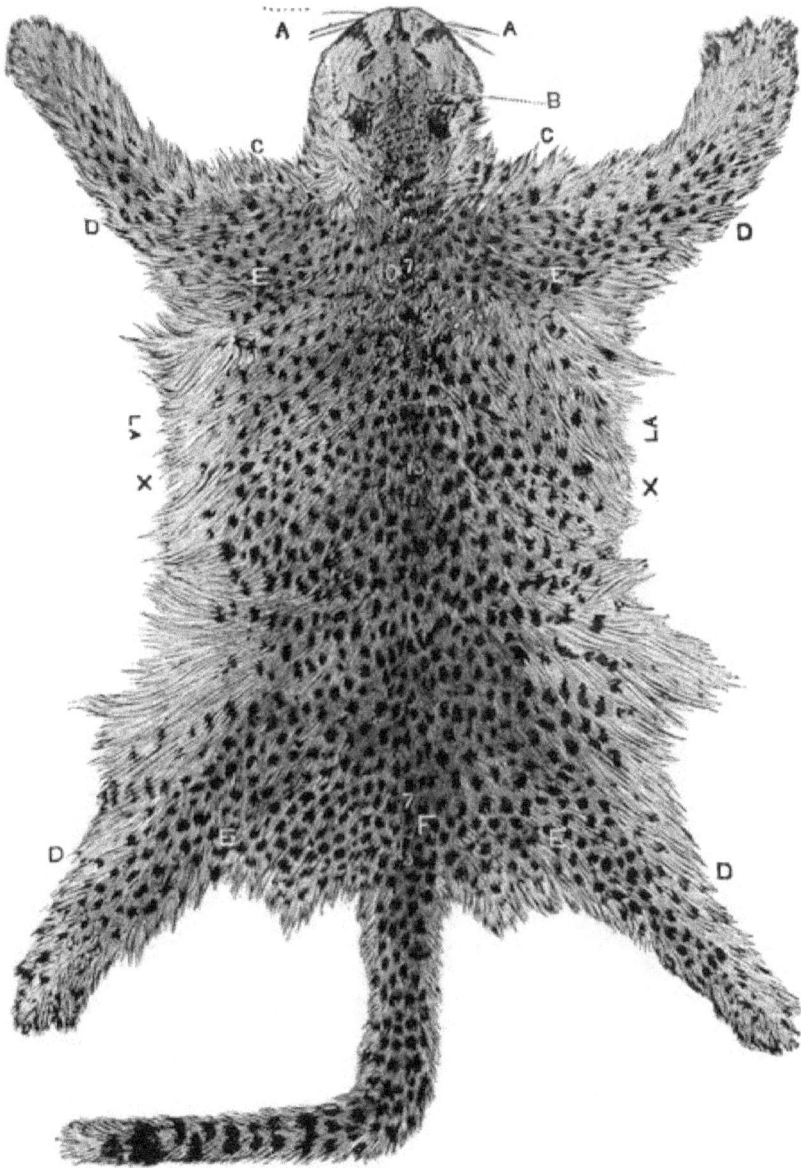

Fig. 13.—Lynx.

The colour changes at the points lettered.

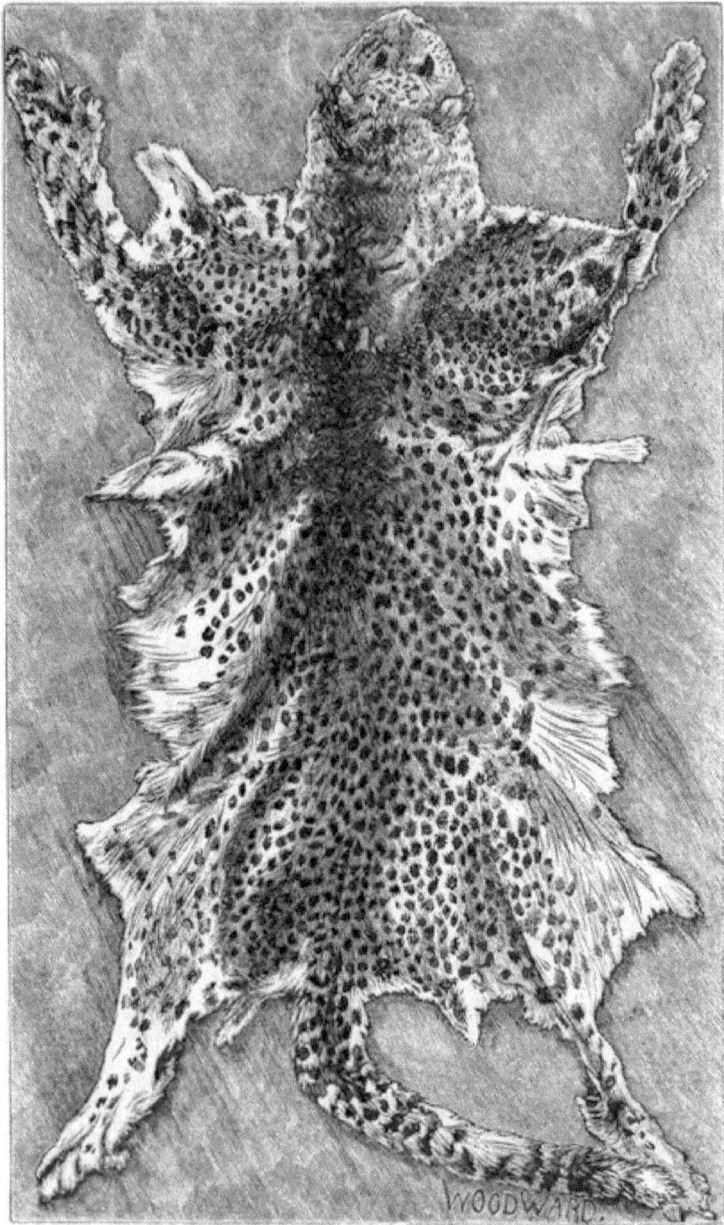

Fig. 14.—LYNX.

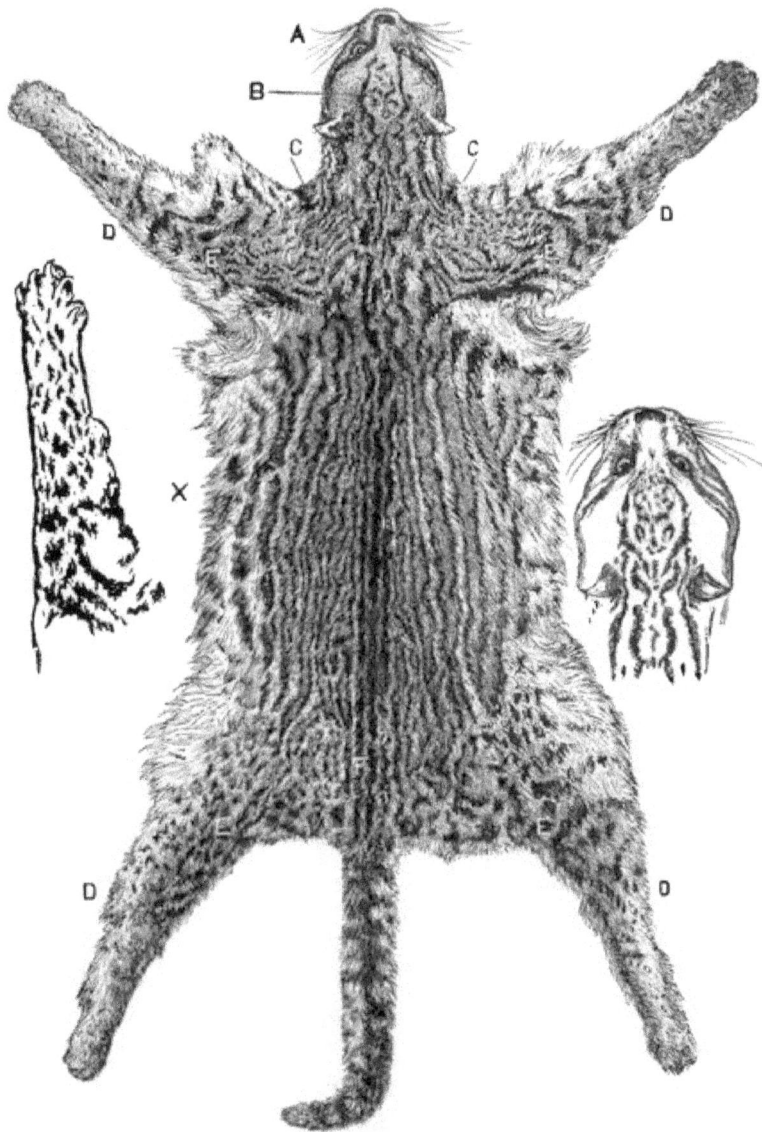

Fig. 15.—OCELOT.

Showing changes of pattern at the joints, &c., with enlargement of head-pattern.

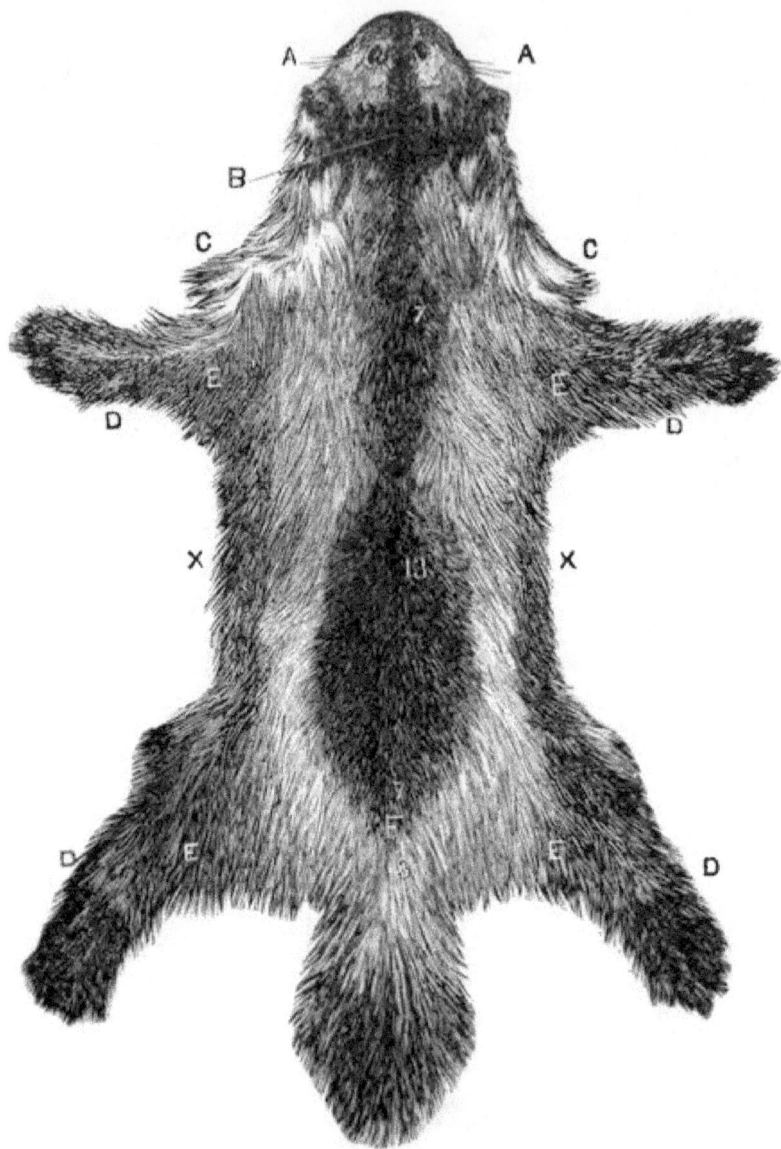

Fig. 16.—BADGER.

The colour changes at the points lettered.

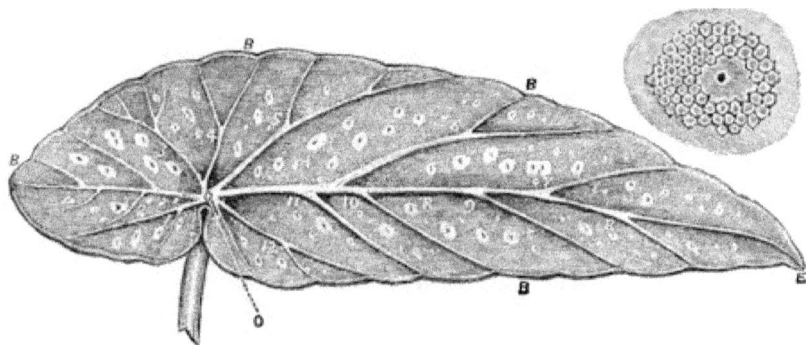

Fig. 17.—BEGONIA LEAF.

www.ingramcontent.com/pod-product-compliance
Lightning Source LLC
Chambersburg PA
CBHW030851270326
41928CB00008B/1319